M000200172

A Psalm-Shaped Life

A Psalm-Shaped Life

H. MARK ABBOTT

WIPF & STOCK · Eugene, Oregon

A PSALM-SHAPED LIFE

Copyright © 2011 H. Mark Abbott. All rights reserved. Except for brief quotations in critical publications or reviews, no part of this book may be reproduced in any manner without prior written permission from the publisher. Write: Permissions, Wipf and Stock Publishers, 199 W. 8th Ave., Suite 3, Eugene, OR 97401.

Primary Scripture translation used is NRSV; secondary translations are NIV and Message.

Wipf & Stock
An Imprint of Wipf and Stock Publishers
199 W. 8th Ave., Suite 3
Eugene, OR 97401

www.wipfandstock.com

ISBN 13: 978-1-61097-421-9

Manufactured in the U.S.A.

Contents

Acknowledgments

M Y HEARTFELT thanks to those who have influenced my life and this book!

I am thankful for the three congregations I have been privileged to serve. This writing is an extension of my calling to ministry, especially to pastoral ministry. I acknowledge my indebtedness to those served at Hamburg Wesleyan Church in suburban Buffalo, New York, College Church in Houghton, New York, but especially First Free Methodist Church of Seattle, where I was lead pastor for twenty-eight years. Many of these reflections on the Psalms were shared with a Wednesday evening class the year before I retired in 2010. I also shared some of these reflections with a midweek group at Rainer Avenue Free Methodist Church in Seattle.

I am thankful for devotional patterns modeled by my father, who loved God and opened his Bible morning after morning as he drank his morning coffee. I have always instinctively known that coffee and Bible go together! Hollis F. Abbott was a missionary and mission administrator, but most of all an expositor of the Word. In the Bible given him at his ordination, which I now possess, the Psalms in particular are well-marked and often dated in the margins.

I am thankful for the one who first turned my eyes from analyzing the Psalms to praying them, Eugene Peterson. I joined large groups who listened to Eugene's lectures at Regent College's Summer School. The spiritual

viii   *Acknowledgments*

formation Peterson wrote and lectured about is based in prayer. And where do we learn to pray? From the Psalms!

Finally, I thank my wife of forty-five years, who has supported and participated in forty-two years of pastoral ministry. Mary Ann knows my need for routine, a routine that regularly includes the Psalms.

1

Psalm-Shaped Lives

Mine and Many

Let the word of Christ dwell in you richly. . . .
Sing psalms, hymns, and spiritual songs to God.
(Col. 3:16)

Sing to him, sing praises to him;
Tell of all his wonderful works. (Ps. 105:2)

ON THE Evergreen Point Bridge across Seattle's Lake Washington, I was on my way to a doctor's appointment. It was a post-surgery follow up several days after a tumor had been removed. The doctor had told me, "It's usually cancer in that location." So I was bracing myself for the "big C" diagnosis. I had already been examined and tested from top to bottom. I'd swallowed dye and had been MRI-ed and CAT-scanned. Now I was prepping myself mentally for cancer treatments and regular testing on into the coming years. And yes, I was apprehensive as I drove to the doctor's office. But into my mind popped a verse from the Psalms, lodged there from frequent readings. It's about "those who fear the Lord." "They shall not be afraid of evil tidings; their hearts are firm, secure in the Lord" (Ps. 112:7). As I allowed this ancient word to echo and re-echo in my mind, I found my spirit quieted and prepared for whatever was ahead.

Several years ago, I was team pastor on a medical mission to Haiti. Because of political instability, our team was going to make a nighttime trip from upcountry to Port au Prince. Our folks were a little shaken by the prospect. I remember calling the group together in a circle and reading Psalm 121. "My help comes from the Lord. . . . He will keep your going out and your coming in now and forever" (Ps. 121:2, 8).

As we navigated burning tire barriers that night and watched heated conversations between the Haitian pastors accompanying us and people with dangerous looking machetes, we remembered, "My help comes from the Lord." Psalm 121 has been called "the traveler's psalm." This vision of God has shaped God's people on their journeys and has given voice to their cries for help.

For more than two decades I have made the Psalms a central part of my regular devotional time. I don't read for quantity but for encounter with God. So I go through all one hundred-fifty psalms at least three times a year. Sometimes when finishing Psalm 150's exciting crescendo, I have said to myself, "You really should read elsewhere in the Bible, you know!" And I have! But sooner or later I come to miss regular exposure to the Psalms. So I return. While I have not set out to memorize very many of the psalms, I find that frequent repetition lodges these powerful words and phrases in my mind. Sometimes at night, awake and unable to return to sleep, I scroll through psalm fragments beginning with successive letters of the alphabet.

ACROSS THREE MILLENNIA, GOD'S PEOPLE HAVE FOUND THEIR LIVES INDIVIDUALLY SHAPED BY THE PSALMS.

This is true from David of Bethlehem to Jesus of Nazareth, from Jerusalem temple worshipers to church people like you and me. The *vision* of believing men and women has been shaped by the Psalms. These ancient prayers have also given believers *voice* to respond to God in the midst of a wide range of life circumstances.

There is good evidence that, on the cross, Jesus was praying the Psalms. Like all good Jews, Jesus must have memorized many of the Psalms. There are echoes of Psalm 22 in what we call "the cry of dereliction": "My God, my God, why have you forsaken me?" (Matt. 27:46). I'm convinced this is not just a theological statement about how a holy God cannot look upon sin being born by God's Son. This is rather an honest cry wrung from one who in those moments of deep suffering and anguish *did feel separated* from God. Jesus voiced this very human anguish in the opening words of Psalm 22. But Jesus also echoed another psalm of lament, which works its way through trouble to trust. "Father, into your hands I commit my spirit" (Ps. 31:5; Luke 23:46). For Jesus, the Psalms gave voice to both anguish and trust.

Throughout most of his life, the Psalms stirred John Wesley, eighteenth-century founder of the Methodist movement. Listening to a St. Paul's Cathedral choir sing Psalm 130 prepared Wesley for his "heart strangely warmed" experience a few hours later in nearby Aldersgate Street. At one point, tempted to doubt his salvation, Wesley found reassurance from the Psalms. "I . . . lifted up my eyes" (Ps. 121:1) and "he sent me help from his holy place" (Ps. 20:2). Experiencing God through the Psalms prompted Wesley to speak of the Psalter as "a rich treasury of devotion."[1] Singing the Psalms, John and Charles Wesley learned, has power "to instruct the community, convey its deepest emotions, and bind it under the lordship of God."[2]

Anatoly Shcharansky was a brilliant young mathematician and chess player. In 1977, at the height of the Cold War, he was arrested by the KGB for repeated attempts to emigrate from the USSR to Israel. Shcharansky spent thirteen years in the Soviet Gulag, where he read and studied all one hundred-fifty psalms in Hebrew. He asked in a letter, "What does this give me?" Answer: "Gradually, my feeling of great loss and sorrow changes to one of bright hopes." Shcharansky's wife, accepting an honorary degree on his behalf, told a university audience, "In a lonely cell in Christopol prison, locked alone with the psalms of David, Anatoly found expression for his innermost feelings in the outpourings of the king of Israel thousands of years ago."[3]

The Psalms are structured into five segments (1–41; 42–72; 73–89; 90–106; 107–150). These divisions mirror the five books of the Torah, leading us to understand the Psalms as God's law in song. Thus the Psalms not only powerfully express human feeling but also provide order for human life. "The unfolding of your words gives light; it imparts understanding to the simple" (Ps. 119:130). The

1. Wesley, "Sermon 103."

2. "Book of Psalms," *Wesley Study Bible*.

3. Yancey, *Bible Jesus Read*, 120.

rest of Psalm 119 describes the impact of God's "words" in shaping and ordering human lives.

A wise American pastor used to offer this prescription to distressed people who came for counsel and comfort: "The twenty-third Psalm, five times a day, for a week. Read or repeat this ancient prayer slowly, savoring its images. Let them shape your vision of God and response to God in the midst of life." Not surprisingly, most people were greatly helped by this simple prescription.

But it's not just the twenty-third Psalm and other comforting prayers that have shaped God's people. In fact, if Psalm 23 is all we know of these ancient prayers, we have missed the wide and varied outpouring of human feeling to God experienced through regular personal and corporate exposure to the Psalms.

There are *psalms of lament*—angry, complaining, questioning, even cursing psalms. Have we found these psalms—according to some estimates, up to seventy percent of the Psalter—expressing what we feel at times of distress, sadness, guilt, and anger? Have we learned how to practice biblical lament?

The psalms we know best are *praise psalms*. Delight in God, which arises out of a healthy relationship with God and enhances that relationship, is expressed in praise. We offer praise for what God does. But we also offer praise for who God is. This is *narrative praise* and *descriptive praise*.

Nature psalms celebrate God's glory in the created world. These psalms do not fall into the error of ancient paganism or contemporary pantheism, that is, of identifying God and nature as one. Thus nature psalms shape not just how we view nature but how we worship God in the context of nature.

There are *storytelling psalms*, which pass on to next generations the individual's story and the great story of what God has done for God's people. Our story shapes the character of our prayers and the character of our whole lives.

In line with the great wisdom literature of the Bible, *wisdom psalms* shape our thoughts and lives especially in such complex areas as death and riches.

Celebration psalms shape our vision and give us voice for times of celebration on our life-pilgrimage.

Hope-shaping psalms lead us to trust in God as "refuge" as we "wait on God." Have images of God as refuge, stronghold, and rock held us firm and given hope in times of turmoil? Psalm-shaped hope sees beyond circumstances to God, chooses against fear, and trusts in God rather than in human resources.

PSALMS ARE NOT ONLY PERSONALLY LIFE-SHAPING BUT HAVE ALSO SHAPED THE CHARACTER OF COMMUNITY WORSHIP DOWN THROUGH THE AGES.

I remember the first time I went on retreat at a Benedictine monastery. When the bell rang, I slipped into the sanctuary, watching as black-robed monks filed into the choir area. Then I was amazed at the impact of chanted psalms washing over my spirit. Monks typically do the entire Psalter in two or three weeks. And they do *all* the psalms, not just the nice, uplifting ones.

Of Gods and Men, a French movie that won second place in the Cannes Film Festival in 2008, is about Trappist monks living with an impoverished Algerian community. In the Algerian Civil War of 1996, under pressure from fundamentalist terrorists, the monks must decide whether to leave or stay. Again and again we watch and listen as the monks turn to God and strengthen their hearts by chanting the Psalms.

Monks today engaging in the regular "hours" of worship five to seven times a day are merely continuing the pattern of worship with the Psalms followed by ancient synagogue worshipers and Christ-followers for the past three thousand years. Through much of history, especially before the printing press was invented, the Psalms were learned by heart and recited in corporate worship. It is said that Pope Gregory the Great refused to consecrate a bishop because this would-be prelate could not recite the whole Psalter. Even the majority of people in past eras, who were not literate, could learn these poetic prayers by listening to them again and again.

The Epistle to the Ephesians urges believers to be filled up not with wine but with the Spirit. They are to express this way of living by using "psalms, hymns, and spiritual songs, singing and making melody to the Lord in your hearts" (Eph. 5:19). Spirit-filling should involve psalm-singing.

For several centuries in English-speaking worship, the only acceptable congregational hymns were psalm paraphrases. It was a major change when eighteenth century hymn writer Isaac Watts began to offer "hymns of human composure," hymns composed by human beings and not merely psalm paraphrases. Today most hymnals and contemporary praise resources are filled with echoes if not direct paraphrases from this hymnbook of God's people.

These days, however, outside of monasteries it's mostly liturgical churches or those that follow a lectionary that regularly use a wide range of psalms in congregational worship. Apart from Psalm-based calls to worship, many evangelical churches seldom give people the privilege of reading from or hearing the Psalms regularly. One accomplishment of mine during twenty-eight years in one parish was to establish the pattern of an every-Sunday congregational Psalm. During Lent we read the penitential psalms. During much of the year we were guided by the lectionary. I must confess I never mustered the courage to insist that we do some of the really angry psalms in corporate worship. But otherwise, we ranged widely through the whole of the Psalms in congregational worship.

So praying the Psalms is not something we only do alone. We also pray the Psalms together. According to Eugene Peterson, "All the psalms are prayers in community: people assembled, attentive before God, participating in a common posture, movement, and speech, offering themselves and each other to their Lord."[4] Prayer, says Peterson, may originate when we are alone, but it matures as it is "integrated into the praying community." In fact, writes Peterson, "Even when we pray the Psalms by ourselves (which most people will do most of the time), we are not by ourselves; community is always implicit in the Psalms, and the moment we pray them, we are drawn into the community."[5]

4. Peterson, *Answering God*, 19.
5. Ibid., 91.

In his introduction to the Psalms from *The Message*, Peterson writes, "Most Christians for most of the Christian centuries have learned to pray by praying the Psalms." The problem, as this wise pastor, professor, and author observes, is that in most of our classic translations, the Psalms sound so literary. "In English translation, the Psalms often sound smooth and polished, sonorous with Elizabethan rhythms and diction. As literature they are beyond compare. But as prayer, as the utterances of men and women passionate for God in moments of anger and praise and lament, these translations miss something. . . . The Psalms in Hebrew are earthy and rough. They are not genteel."

So, Peterson began paraphrasing psalms into the rhythms and diction of contemporary English. "I wanted to provide men and women access to the terrific energies of prayer in the kind of language that is most immediate to them, which also happens to be the language in which these psalm prayers were first expressed and written by David and his successors."[6]

Whether in the contemporary language of *The Message* or in the words of more traditional translations, the Psalms need to be heard and read together by God's people in our regular gatherings for worship.

WHAT IS "A PSALM-SHAPED LIFE?"

In this book I will make the case that a psalm-shaped life is:

- One in which the Psalms' *vision* of God shapes us through personal and corporate worship and

6. Peterson, "Introduction."

- one in which the Psalms' outpouring of wide-ranging emotions gives *voice* to our personal and corporate prayers.

A psalm-shaped life intentionally develops the habit of immersing ourselves in the prayer book of God's ancient people and of Christ-followers in the past two millennia. The vision and voice of these ancient prayers regularly incorporated into our own devotional lives and into our congregational worship cannot help but shape twenty-first-century men and women even as they have God's people for the past three thousand years.

TOWARD PSALM-SHAPED LIVING, BOTH INDIVIDUALLY AND CORPORATELY, I OFFER THE FOLLOWING SUGGESTIONS:

For some, these may be life changes; for others, reinforcement of what you already do. The final chapter in this book will flesh out these brief suggestions.

Read the Psalms daily, slowly, and prayerfully.

Read them all, from Psalm 1 to 150. But when in need of a renewed vision of God or a voice with which to respond to God and to life, turn to particular psalms that respond to your felt need. "Out of the depths I cry to You, O Lord!" (Ps. 130:1) has been my prayer in times of distress and after failure. "The traveler's psalm" (Ps. 121) has preceded group journeys: "The Lord will keep your going out and your coming in" (v. 8).

Pray the Psalms.

Many psalms can be offered in prayer as they are. Many can become our prayers with slight adaptation. Let the voice of the psalmist launch us further into our own prayers. I have recently taken to writing my own prayers that reflect on one or more of the morning's psalms.

Let the language of the Psalms become our language of prayer.

Let the psalmists' prayers become our voice for responding to God in the midst of life. Let this be so even with angry, bitter psalms and self-righteous sounding, self-vindicating psalms. Let all of life be poured out before the One who has remarkable tolerance for radical variations in our responses to God and to life. Let psalm fragments repeated again and again nurture a Godward vision and trust in God by day and by night. I have recently been using Psalm 63:8 this way: "My soul clings to you; your right hand upholds me."

Move toward regular psalm reading in small- and large-group worship gatherings.

If it is not already practiced where you worship, encourage psalm reading in worship. Let the Psalms renew our vision of God together and give us voice to speak together to this God who is open to our cries in all of life. Let modern believers and the contemporary church return to the consistent spirit-shaping of the Psalter.

Join me in revisiting what these ancient prayers were to those who first used the Psalms. Join me in exploring how the psalmists' vision of God, creation, suffering, and evil may more completely shape and form our lives and then give us voice to respond back to God in the midst of every imaginable situation. At the end of each chapter, I will share my own psalm-based prayers. But because we learn how to hear and pray the Psalms by understanding their language rhythms, the following chapter will investigate some of the patterns of ancient Hebrew poetry.

But before we go on, return with me to my post-op doctor's visit with which I began this chapter. There was the usual wait to see the specialist. I busied myself leafing through magazines I don't usually spend time with—you know the kind you find in waiting rooms! As I waited, those words from the Psalms continued to shape my outlook. "They shall not be afraid of evil tidings; their hearts are firm, secure in the Lord" (Ps. 112:7).

Finally the busy doctor was ready to see me. "I've got good news for you!" he said. "Surprisingly, the tumor is not malignant." And he went on to describe the relatively rare benign tissue removed from my body. No, the outcome of a doctor's visit is not always so positive. Just as the sun rises on the evil and the good (Matt. 5:45), so cancer is diagnosed among believers and nonbelievers. But even in the midst of bad news and hard times, the Psalms have shaped the outlook and response of God's people.

PRAYING FROM PSALM 23

Thank you, Great Shepherd, that in you I am never in want.

You lead me, guide me, and provide for me.

You are present to comfort me even in times of deep darkness.

You host me at your banquet table.

You invite me to live with you forever.

But today, I revel in this reality: you restore my soul.

Yesterday's distress, today's sense of heaviness is not forever.

But in you there is restoration of health in my inner being.

So today I leave with you whatever distresses me and leads me into a heavy spirit.

Today, I open myself to your restoration of soul.

Today, Great Shepherd, I walk within your care.

Amen!

2

So What's a Psalm?

Sing psalms and hymns and spiritual songs among yourselves, singing and making melody to the Lord in your hearts. (Eph. 5:19)

It is good to give thanks to the Lord,
To sing praises to your name, O Most High;
To declare your steadfast love in the morning,
And your faithfulness by night. (Ps. 92:1–2)

THOUGH IT may be just an urban legend, I have heard that the two most recognizable expressions worldwide are "Coca-Cola" and "hallelujah." I have imbibed Coke on four continents. And on lips of believers both individually and together I've heard repeated cries of "Hallelujah!" on those same four continents. Listen to whispered prayers of individuals worldwide and to jubilant voices raised in praise and you will hear "Hallelujah! Hallelujah!" Recently in the "warm heart of Africa," in Malawi, amid hymns and choruses in the Chechewa language, I heard frequent renditions of "Hallelujah!"

PSALMS ARE HALLELUJAHS, PRAISES TO GOD.

Hallelujah is Hebrew for "praise be to Jah," which is short for Yahweh, God. The Hebrew Bible's name for what we call the Psalms is *tehillim*, which comes from the same root word as hallelujah. The Greek word *psalmoi* means "songs sung to a harp," or just "songs of praise." *Psalterium* is the Latin word behind the word "psalter," a name often given to the Book of Psalms, and refers to a zither-like stringed instrument popular in medieval Europe. In English Bibles, the title "Psalms" is attached to this central and life-shaping book.

PSALMS MAY FEEL DISTANT FROM US.

Some of the psalms are easy for contemporary folks to get happy about. Some are not. Some are downright confusing. Biblical scholar Tremper Longman III has pointed out three areas of distance between us and the Psalms. Making the case that contemporary believers and believing communities ought to be psalm-shaped in their vision of and response to God does not eliminate these areas of distance.

First, the Psalms are *chronologically distant*. The most recent psalm was written about twenty-five hundred years ago, the earliest possibly thirty-five hundred years ago. Since "God speaks to his people in ways and through means related to their own times," these ancient song-prayers can feel distant. The first psalms are probably from the time of Homer, the Greek epic poet, whose writings feel very distant from most of us.

Second, the Psalms are *culturally distant*. They were not written first of all for us but for ancient Middle Easterners, the people of Israel. "We can expect that we will run into customs and expressions that are strange to our modern, technological society." Brutally frank expressions of feeling may be distressing for Western Christians schooled in "right ways" to pray.[1]

Finally, at least some of the Psalms feel *theologically distant*. They were written before Christ and are based in temple worship and in animal sacrifice, which is quite different from the world of twenty-first-century Christians.

Popular Scottish novelist Alexander McCall Smith has Jamie, one of his characters, comment on when he was a choirboy and found it hard not to laugh at Old Testament readings. "We found the Old Testament screamingly funny at that age. All that smiting!" Isabel, heroine of McCall's Edinburgh series, responds, "And begetting . . . boys must find talk of begetting very amusing."[2]

I sit in a busy, glassed-in food court in a major airport, watching the parade of planes outside and the parade of humanity inside. Most of the people I watch are connecting digitally. The technology driving huge planes launching or landing in my vision and the microtechnology of computers and cell phones to which people are attached is millennia away from the Psalms. At the same time, emotions on people's faces as they process information on laptops and carry on conversation via cell phone would have been recognizable by these ancient poets. As I eavesdrop on conversations, I hear excitement and joy but also stress and distress,

1. Longman, *How to Read the Psalms*, 14.
2. Smith, *Charming Quirks of Others*, 69.

frustration and anger, fear and sadness. Occasionally in these huge concourses you see folks in obvious grief and sadness. Into some lives has come deep loss. The journeys that bring these people to the airport are not happy ones.

Today's human experience is worlds apart from three thousand years ago. But human emotions of today are remarkably similar to those honestly and openly expressed by the psalmists. Give powerful phrases from the psalms to some of the travelers I watch and overhear and many would agree, "Wow! That's just how I feel!"

And the God before whom we live our lives is the same yesterday, today, and forever. This God was and is not detached, immune from human emotions like a computer-induced voice. This personal God is still good, loving, strong, faithful, compassionate, hope-giving, and worthy of being praised and worshiped.

Thus, with some background understanding and a heart open to encountering God through the Psalms, these ancient song-prayers can be life-shaping to those who will immerse themselves in their powerful flow. The trouble is that most people within my airport purview know little or nothing about the Psalms. And sadly, so it is with multitudes of believers who claim to believe the Bible but have not immersed themselves in the wide stream of prayer and song we find in the Psalms. The distance between us and these ancient prayers keeps many from being shaped and formed by the Psalms' vision of God and their voice with which to respond to God and to life.

But again, what's a psalm? Let's not get technical or academic, yet let's review some basic information about the Psalms. Understanding what these ancient poets were doing may begin to bridge the distance between us and the psalmists.

PSALMS ARE HEBREW POETRY.

That being so, we don't expect to read and interpret the Psalms the same way as we do, for example, the Epistles of Paul. Literary genre is huge when we read any literature, the Bible included. When we come to a Shakespearean sonnet or a Japanese haiku, we need to know something about how this kind of literature works. So it is with the poetry of the Psalms.

As Hebrew poetry, psalms are *image rich*. According to Kathleen Norris, "The psalms do not theologize. . . . One reason for this is that the psalms are poetry, and poetry's function is not to explain but to offer images and stories that resonate with our lives."[3]

Psalm images come out of the ancient Middle East and thus are highly symbolic. We don't take the ancient poet literally when he sings, "He will cover you with his pinions ["feathers" NIV], and under his wings you will find refuge. . . . You will tread on the lion and the adder, the young lion and the serpent you will trample under foot" (Ps. 91:4).

Just think of the multiple images used in the Psalms to speak of God. God is shield, fortress, rock, storm cloud, shepherd, warrior, archer, chariot-rider, king. These many images begin to shape a picture in our minds and hearts of what God is like. Pictures speak to our emotions, not just to our intellects. Pictures involve mystery. And when we deal with God and with life, there is always mystery.

3. Quoted in Yancey, *Bible Jesus Read*, 69.

As we have already observed, image-rich Scripture may be complicated for us to respond to because many of the images are drawn from millennia ago and a culture very different than our own. Occasionally the psalmist will even use an ancient mythological allusion. For example, in Psalm 48, Zion, the mountain on which the temple was built, is compared with Zaphon, the imposing mythological mountain where pagan god Baal was thought to dwell. "Like the utmost heights of Zaphon is Mount Zion, the city of the great king" (Ps. 48:2 NIV).

Zaphon was a place fit for a powerful god. That doesn't mean the poet buys into what that mythology depicts about Baal and his dwelling place. It does mean the poet is using the image to paint a picture and thus communicate with the people of his time. Yahweh is the true God. Baal is not.

Another key characteristic of Hebrew poetry is *parallelism*. Instead of rhyming words, as in "Twinkle, twinkle, little star / How I wonder what you are . . . ," ancient Hebrews used parallel word structures. In temple worship, these parallel segments may well have been used antiphonally, somewhat like today's responsive readings.

Parallel phrases or lines may be *synonymous*. In other words, the second phrase or line repeats the same thought in somewhat different language.

> O Lord, who may abide in your tent?
> Who may dwell on your holy hill? (Ps. 15:1)
>
> His delight is in the law of the Lord;
> On his law he meditates day and night. (Ps. 1:2)

Some parallelism may be *antithetic*. The second part of the parallelism contrasts with or is the opposite of what is expressed in the first part.

> For the Lord watches over the way of the righteous,
> but the way of the wicked will perish. (Ps. 1:6)

Or the parallelism may be *synthetic*, that is, the second and maybe third lines complete what the first line is saying.

> The voice of the Lord causes the oaks to whirl,
> and strips the forest bare;
> and in his temple all say, "Glory!" (Ps. 29:9)

Scholars expand the categories of parallelism to account for what they see in the Psalms. But I think we get the basic idea. However, you might say, "So what? What difference does that make?"

At times in Hebrew poetry, it is important for our understanding to know that a following line explains, expands, or completes the first line. In Psalm 63:8 the ancient poet prays,

> My soul clings to you;
> Your right hand upholds me.

I hear this synthetic parallelism telling me that "clinging to" God (my responsibility) goes together with God's right hand upholding me (God's part). All day and into the night I can affirm my responsibility while trusting that God will act in accord with who God is. Maybe it's like a common paraphrase from St. Augustine: "Without us God will not. Without God, we cannot."

Let me use an illustration outside the Psalms but still in the genre of Hebrew poetry. A key segment of the first creation account given us in Genesis 1 is obviously poetic.

> So God created humankind in his image,
> In the image of God he created them. . . .
> Male and female he created them. (Gen. 1:27)

The second line is parallel to and synonymous with the first. But the third line is synthetic and draws out the meaning of the first two lines. Thus there must be something about the image of God expressed in human maleness and femaleness. Without this clue given in the parallelism of Hebrew poetry, we might miss a key interpretive insight.

A further characteristic of Hebrew poetry is the *acrostic*. In an acrostic the first word of each line or of each grouping of lines begins with a successive letter of the Hebrew alphabet. Psalms 9, 10, 25, 34, 37, 111, 112, and 145 are acrostics. But the classic illustration of acrostic is Psalm 119. Each segment of this marathon psalm begins with a new letter in the Hebrew alphabet.

Remember that the Psalms came out of an oral and aural culture. Speaking and hearing, not primarily writing and reading, were the means of communication. Stop and think of what it would mean only to hear and not to be able to read Psalms—or any Scripture, for that matter. Acrostic may have been one of the devices used to aid both hearing and memorization. It doesn't help us, but it does help us to understand why they used this literary device.

PSALMS ARE HEBREW POETRY SET TO MUSIC.

The authors of *The Bible for Dummies* put it this way: "Imagine the lyrics to your favorite songs without the music—fairly empty in comparison (especially the ooh baby's). Thus, when ancient Israelites stood before God to express their emotions, they set their prayers to music."[4]

Some psalm headings may be musical instructions regarding what tune to use. "According to the Dove on Far-off Terebinths" (56) probably indicates a familiar tune. "*Shiggaion*" preceding Psalm 7 may direct attention to an irregular meter. Other psalms are directed to be used "with stringed instruments" (67).

WHERE DID THE PSALMS COME FROM?

Seventy-three of the one hundred-fifty psalms are ascribed to David. The poet-king was known as "the sweet singer of Israel," or "Israel's singer of songs" (2 Sam. 23:1 NIV). Several of the David psalms have historical headings, noting events in David's life out of which the psalm came. For example, the heading of Psalm 56 references the time when Philistines seized David in Gath (1 Sam. 21:10–15). The heading of the next psalm describes the time when "he fled from Saul, in the cave" (1 Sam. 24). The intensely penitential Psalm 51 is headed "When the prophet Nathan came to him, after he had gone in to Bathsheba" (1 Sam. 11–12).

Other psalms are ascribed to Korah (42–47) and Asaph (73–83). These were temple worship leaders. A section of Psalms between numbers 120 and 134 are labeled

4. Geoghegan and Homan, *Bible for Dummies*, 229.

"psalms of ascent." These were probably sung by pilgrims ascending to Jerusalem for festival occasions. "Hallelujah psalms" (113–18) are linked historically with the festivals of Passover and Tabernacles.

But move beyond literary and historical dimensions of the Psalms, and most basically *psalms are prayers expressing the full range of human response to God.* These ancient prayers are sometimes wrung from hearts of people in distress. They are the expression of something very deep in our experience.

> Deep calls to deep at the thunder of your cataracts;
> All your wave sand your billows have gone over. . . .
> I say to God, my rock,
> "Why have you forgotten me?"
> Why must I walk about mournfully
> Because the enemy oppresses me. . . .
> Why are you cast down, O my soul,
> And why are you disquieted within me?
> But out of this deep place of disquiet, comes the cry
> of hope and trust.
> Hope in God; for I shall again praise him,
> My help and my God. (Ps. 42:7–11)

Psalm 55 involves some of the most radical mood swings in the Psalms. The ancient poet, maybe David, has been betrayed by a trusted friend. He is terribly troubled by this. And he wants to escape and get away from it all. "Fear and trembling come upon me, and horror overwhelms me. And I say 'O that I had wings like a dove! I would fly away and be at rest'" (Ps. 55:6–7).

Does that register a responsive chord in us? Have we felt betrayed, in anguish, wanting to escape? But David's response comes back to who God is and what God will do. "Cast your burden on the Lord, and he will sustain you; he will never permit the righteous to be moved" (Ps. 55:22).

BECAUSE THESE PRAYERS EXPRESS THE FULL RANGE OF HUMAN RESPONSES TO GOD, THEY ARE WIDELY VARIED IN KIND.

As already observed, Psalms includes *lament*, human sorrow poured out to God. Laments may reflect a community in crisis, such as in Psalm 80, or an individual crisis, as in Psalm 13. (See chapter 6 for more on psalms of lament.)

On the opposite pole of human emotion, Psalms include *praises*, involving joy spoken to God. This may be narrative praise, or response to the great acts of God. These may take the form of community praise, such as in Psalm 124, and the "royal psalms," such as Psalm 47. Or they may be individual praise, illustrated powerfully by Psalm 30.

Praise psalms are "narrative praise," telling the story of delight in what God has done. But praise psalms are also "descriptive praise," responding to and describing who God is. They describe the character of God, such as in Psalm 113. (See chapter 5 for more on psalms of praise.)

Other categories of the Psalms include *celebration psalms or liturgies*, worship in action and speech as illustrated in Psalm 24. (See chapter 8.) Another category is the *wisdom psalms*, comprising wise meditations on life, as in Psalms 1 and 49. (See chapter 9.) There are also *storytelling psalms*. (See chapter 4.) And there are *nature psalms*, which celebrate the beauty of God's natural creation. (See chapter 3.) These varied kinds of psalms cover the whole gamut of human experience, giving us a vision of God in all of life and voice to respond to God in the midst of life.

One more word about what Psalms are.

PSALMS ARE THE CORPORATE HYMNBOOK OF GOD'S ANCIENT PEOPLE—AND OURS TOO.

Frequently the psalmists describe their participation in the community's worship.

> I will enter your house,
> I will bow down towards your holy temple
> In awe of you. (Ps. 5:7)

> I will come into your house with burnt-offering;
> I will pay you my vows. (Ps. 66:13)

> I have looked upon you in the sanctuary,
> Beholding your power and glory. (Ps. 63:2)

Psalms are not merely private musings. Psalms are the corporate worship of God's ancient people. We are the poorer if we do not incorporate these ancient song-prayers into the worship of our faith communities. In today's congregational worship, branching outside the friendly and happy psalms may at times require setting the stage and developing the context so contemporary worshipers can understand. But this is how God's ancient people worshiped God. Surely the Psalms can and should give vision and voice to our worship thousands of years later.

But enough *about* the Psalms! We jump now into this life-changing stream. I hope you will join me in reading the

Psalms regularly if not daily. This is not just an academic exercise but an invitation to be shaped and formed by God.

ALLOW GOD TO SHAPE YOUR LIFE BY THE PSALMS.

- Find a quiet time and place and pause to prepare your heart, inviting God to communicate with you.

- Read one or two psalms depending on their length. Read slowly, trying to identify with the emotion being poured out to God. Maybe a word or phrase will jump out at you. Savor that insight on God. Incorporate that voice for communicating with God into your own prayers.

- Go back once more and pray the psalm. Let its words and images lead you into your own open and honest responses to God. Maybe you will want to put your own reflections on your psalm reading into a prayer. At endings, I incorporate some of my own prayers from reading the Psalms.

- Use Psalms together when God's people gather in small or large groups for worship. Let these corporate prayers shape not only our individual lives, but our lives together.

Philip Yancey, who confesses to struggling with the Psalms much of his life, came to a life-shaping encounter with these ancient prayer-songs. "From Psalms," writes Yancey, "I have learned that I can rightfully bring to God *whatever* I feel about him. I need not paper over my failures and try to clean up my own rottenness; far better to bring those weaknesses to God, who alone has the power to heal."[5]

PRAYING FROM PSALMS 20–21 (PSALMS ABOUT THE KING AND VICTORY)

Great God, you are the King, King of David, King of me, King of all that is.

In your name, because of who you are, there is protection, help, support.

You grant my heart's desire and fulfill my petitions, leading me to shout for joy and unfurl banners of celebration.

You bestow blessings and make me glad with the joy of your presence.

Lord God, our King, it is easy to revert and default to taking pride in and trusting in chariots and horses, in human resources and power. But I choose to trust in your Name, Lord, my God.

I want to trust in you, believing that as I rely on and live in your steadfast love, I will not be moved or shaken or in turmoil.

You are exalted, O Lord, in your kingly strength!

I will sing and praise your power!

Amen!

5. Yancey, *Bible Jesus Read*, 122.

3

A Psalm-Shaped Vision of God and Nature

> God saw everything that he had made, and in-
> deed, it was very good. (Gen. 1:31)

> Lord, how manifold are your works. . . .
> When you send forth your spirit, they are created;
> And you renew the face of the earth. (Ps. 104:24, 30)

RECENTLY, MY wife and I drove from Seattle to Sunrise, the northeastern corner of Mount Rainier National Park. It was a pristine Pacific Northwest day. "The Mountain," as Northwesterners call it, was out in full splendor. Trails around Sunrise were still snow-covered in early July. But as we slogged through soft snow we were consistently captured by magnificent vistas of this beautiful mountain. Mount Rainier loomed everywhere we looked.

When we moved to Seattle I began to realize why ancient people thought the gods lived on the top of mountains. Much of the year Mount Rainier seems like a figment of the Chamber of Commerce's imagination. Cloud-covered and mysterious, she is often hidden from view. But when the majestic, glacier-draped peak appears, she seems to spread a blessing over the whole region. Even the most cynical and jaded of urban dwellers pauses to reflect on the wonder of Mount Rainier on a clear day.

Again and again, that day at Sunrise on the slopes of Mount Rainier, the classic hymn ran through my mind:

> I sing the mighty power of God, that made the mountains rise,
> That spread the glowing seas abroad and built the lofty skies . . .
> Lord, how thy wonders are displayed, where'er I turn my eye,
> When I survey the ground I tread, or gaze upon the sky.

While not strictly a Psalm paraphrase, hymn writer Isaac Watts was drawing on psalm imagery.

> The Lord is a great God, and a great King above all gods.
> In His hand are the depths of the earth;
> the heights of the mountains are his also.
> The sea is His, for He made it,
> And the dry land, which His hands have formed.
> (Ps. 95:3–5)

In Seattle, we are surrounded by mountains and water. From the deck at our home, I can see glimpses of Elliott Bay. When I walk in Discovery Park, there's the wider expanse of Puget Sound. When the "marine layer" lifts, the blue sky sings of beauty and majesty. Seattle is one of America's beautiful cities. But wherever we live, we can celebrate the wonderful world of nature. Each varied kind of scenery has its own special beauty. And every kind of scenery points to the God who created it all. The Psalmist sings, "The heavens are telling the glory of God. Day to day pours forth speech, and night to night declares knowledge" (Ps. 19:1–2).

We begin our immersion in these spirit-shaping psalms by listening to and praying the great psalms that celebrate God's wonderful natural creation.

When he looked at the world of nature, the psalmists' thoughts turned to God.

> I think about all of your deeds;
> I meditate on the works of your hands. (Ps. 143:5)

> How manifold are your works;
> In wisdom you have made them all. (Ps. 104:24)

Or hear it in Eugene Peterson's *The Message*: "What a wildly wonderful world, GOD! You made it all, with Wisdom at your side, made earth overflow with your wonderful creations."

Psalm 8 is sometimes called "The Midnight Psalm."

> O Lord, our Sovereign, how majestic is your name in
> all the earth!
> You have set your glory above the heavens.
> Out of the mouths of babes and infants
> you have founded a bulwark because of your foes,
> to silence the enemy and the avenger.
> When I look at your heavens, the work of your fingers,
> the moon and the stars that you have established;
> what are human beings that you are mindful of them,
> mortals that you care for them? (Ps. 8:1–4)

For obvious reasons, Psalm 19 is sometimes known as "The Sunrise Psalm."

> In the heavens he has set a tent for the sun,
> which comes out like a bridegroom from his wedding
> canopy,
> and like a strong man runs its course with joy.
> Its rising is from the end of the heavens, and its circuit
> to the end of them;
> and nothing is hid from its heat. (Ps. 19:4–6)

Psalm 19 pairs "the light without and the light within," God revealed in nature and God revealed in the Law. Both combine to speak God's glory and move us to prayer.

Psalm 29 has been named "The Psalm of the Seven Thunders."

> The voice of the Lord is over the waters;
> the God of glory thunders, the Lord, over mighty waters.
> The voice of the Lord is powerful;
> the voice of the Lord is full of majesty.
> The voice of the Lord breaks the cedars;
> the Lord breaks the cedars of Lebanon.
> He makes Lebanon skip like a calf, and Sirion like a
> young wild ox.
> The voice of the Lord flashes forth flames of fire.
> The voice of the Lord shakes the wilderness;
> the Lord shakes the wilderness of Kadesh.
> The voice of the Lord causes the oaks to whirl, and
> strips the forest bare. (Ps. 29:4–6)

Read and revel in praise to God from all of nature as celebrated in Psalm 104. From the heavens "stretched out like a tent," to the clouds as God's chariot, riding "on the wings of the wind," all of nature combines to "bless the Lord" and sing, "O Lord my God, you are very great, you are clothed with honor and majesty" (Ps. 104:1).

"The theater of the glory of God" is the way theologian Alister McGrath speaks of nature.[1] "Creation," writes Eugene Peterson, "is our place for meeting God and conversing with him. . . . We take box seats in this creation theater when we pray. We look around. The mountains are huge, heaving their bulk upwards. The creeks spill across the rocks, giving extravagant light shows under the hemlocks. The lakes fill up with sky, on earth as it is in heaven."[2]

The psalmists belonged to a nation of peasant-farmers, who lived close to the soil. "What they give us," wrote C. S. Lewis, "is the very feel of weather—weather seen with a real countryman's eyes, enjoyed almost as a vegetable might be supposed to enjoy it."[3] The Psalms come out of the ancient Middle East where rain was a vital and precious thing. These people knew about real deserts, where thirst was an ever present reality and rain was indeed a gift of God. People who lived in the water-starved Judean highlands or nearby Judean wilderness knew what the psalmist meant when he cried out, "As the deer longs for flowing streams, so my soul longs for you, O God. My soul thirsts for God, for the Living God" (Ps. 42:1–2).

And from another Psalm that is filled with nature imagery:

> You visit the earth and water it,
> You greatly enrich it. . . .
> You water its furrow abundantly, settling its ridges,
> Softening it with showers, and blessing its growth.
> You crown the year with your bounty,

1. McGrath, *Passionate Intellect*, 71.

2. Peterson, *Answering God*, 71.

3. Lewis, *Reflections on the Psalms*, 77.

Your wagon tracks overflow with richness.
(Ps. 65:9–11)

And yes, these are pre-scientific people who did not know about "the laws of nature" described by modern science. When it rained, God sent it. When there was drought, God did it. When it thundered, God was speaking. When crops grew or when they did not, God was responsible.

In my part of the world, many mistake nature for God. We hear a lot about "Mother Nature." "Spiritual" people feel a kinship with the higher power they see in the mountains and trees, leaping salmon, rushing streams, and the icy power of a glacier.

BUT IN THE PSALMS, NATURE IS A TESTIMONY TO GOD RATHER THAN THE DIRECT PRESENCE OF GOD.

Markedly different from popular Western spirituality, which is deeply pantheistic, the Psalms see God as Creator, not as one with the creation. God and the beautiful Madrona trees nearby are not one and the same. God and Mount Rainier, or God and the lion we saw recently in a South African game park, are not one and the same. We do not worship nature but allow nature to point us to God. Yes, God is present in nature. But nature testifies to God rather than being God itself. In Psalm 19, "The Sunrise Psalm," the sun is not a god of order as in surrounding cultures. Rather, the psalmist gives witness to God's powerful and beautiful ordering of nature.

C. S. Lewis put it this way: "Nature and God were distinct; the One had made the other; the One ruled and the other obeyed. . . . To say that God created Nature, while it brings God and Nature into relation, also separates them. What makes and what is made must be two, not one. Thus, the doctrine of Creation in one sense empties Nature of divinity."[4]

> THUS OUR INTEREST IN THESE PSALMS IS NOT SO MUCH WHAT THEY SAY ABOUT NATURE BUT WHAT NATURE REVEALS ABOUT GOD.

"Nature," writes theologian Alister McGrath, "does not prove God's existence; yet the existence of God may be held to be the best explanation of what is actually observed."[5] And these nature psalms illustrate how we can worship God in the context of nature or with the wonderful world of nature in mind.

We love to sing along with Swedish hymn writer Gustav Boberg. This pastor and member of Parliament was enjoying a bayside walk when a thunderstorm appeared out of nowhere. When the severe wind ceased, Boberg looked out over the clear bay. He heard a church bell in the distance. Words formed in his heart and mind and became the much loved hymn "How Great Thou Art." Nature turned the heart and mind of this hymnwriter to worship God.

4. Ibid., 77.
5. McGrath, *Passionate Intellect*, 80.

BUT WHAT CAN NATURE NOT TELL US ABOUT GOD?

Nature cannot sing of "steadfast love and mercy," of forgiveness, healing, and redemption. Nature cannot sing the oft repeated Old Testament stanza about God:

> The Lord is merciful and gracious,
> Slow to anger and abounding in steadfast love.
> He will not always accuse, nor will he keep his anger for ever.
> He does not deal with us according to our sins,
> Nor repay us according to our iniquities. (Ps. 103:8–10)

Nature cannot sing of God's justice and special concern for the oppressed, as does the same Psalm 103: "The Lord works vindication and justice for all who are oppressed" (Ps. 103:6).

Nature, as we see it today, not only points to God but to the created world's present distress caused by human sin. As McGrath observes, "Nature remains God's creation but is now profoundly ambiguous, signaling both its divine origins and its present distress."[6]

Fortunately, nature is not the only vision of God we have. Jesus is the supreme vision of who God is and what God is like. Jesus incarnates the loving heart of God, which nature cannot show us.

BUT TO WHAT DO NATURE PSALMS POINT US?

A psalm-shaped life envisions *a God of majesty and power*. Before this majestic and powerful God, we bow humbly,

6. Ibid., 76.

recognizing how small we really are. Nature psalms call us to "bow down" and to "bless the Lord." Nature psalms help us see ourselves as small but valued by the Creator God. "Ascribe to the Lord glory and strength . . . worship the Lord in holy splendor" (Ps. 29:1–2).

> When I look at your heavens, the work of your fingers,
> the moon and the stars that you have established,
> what are human being that you are mindful of them,
> mortals that you care for them? (Ps. 8:3–4)

A psalm-shaped life envisions *God as Lord over all creation*. God is Lord over all because God is creator of all. God is owner of all creation because God is Creator.

> The Lord is a great God,
> And a great King above all gods.
> In his hand are the depths of the earth,
> The heights of the mountains are his also.
> The seas is his, for he made it,
> And the dry land, which his hands have formed.
> (Ps. 95:3–5)

Even we as human beings belong to God. We are God's. Why? Because God created us! And we take our place with all created things in our dependence on our Lord God, Creator and Owner. "It is he that made us, and we are his, we are his people and the sheep of his pasture" (Ps. 100:3).

C. S. Lewis observes that in Psalm 104, lions and whales exist side by side with men and men's cattle (Ps. 104:21–23). Lewis writes: "We all—lions, storks, ravens, whales—live, as our fathers said, 'as God's charges,' and the mention of all equally redounds to His praise."[7]

7. Lewis, *Reflections on the Psalms*, 85.

A psalm-shaped life also envisions *a God of beauty and creativity*. Think of the grand beauty of creation—Mount Rainier, the Grand Canyon, the Pacific Ocean, the Antarctic ice field, the vastness of space and its planets. But think also of little things, beauty we can hold in the palms of our hands—birds, butterflies, a baby's fingers. Just imagine: "It was you who formed my inward parts, you knit me together in my mother's womb. I praise you for I am fearfully and wonderfully made. Wonderful are your works" (Ps. 139:13–14).

On a recent safari in Malawi, Africa's Liwonde National Park, we were stunned at the bright colors of small birds feeding alongside powerful crocodiles, hippos, and elephants. The Creator God celebrated in nature psalms is a God of beauty and creativity.

Nature psalms shape our vision of who God is.

BUT WHAT KEEPS US FROM CELEBRATING GOD'S GLORY IN NATURE?

Do we sometimes miss pointers to God in nature? Are we so busy that we overlook beauty, both big and small?

Forty years ago I saw a church sign I have not forgotten. "How long since you saw a sunset?" It wasn't just a question about whether we looked westward when the sun went down but whether we really *saw* a sunset. Do flaming colors of the setting sun move us to worship? Or do we think, "That's nice!" take a quick picture, and move on?

Maui Sunset, an oceanside condo, is where we have spent vacation time courtesy of a friend's generosity. Daily sunsets in front of the condo building are marked by the blowing of a conch shell, taking pictures, and rating this sunset over another, but seldom by prayer. To enjoy beauty is not the same as praising God the Creator of beauty.

I'm a morning walker. In spring and summer, streets in our neighborhood are lined with blooming flowers. But do I pause to look and turn my heart to God in praise and worship? Sometimes I catch myself striding along, deep in some profound thought, missing the amazing beauty around me.

Elizabeth Barrett Browning wrote:

> Earth's cramm'd with heaven,
> And every common bush aglow with God.
> But only he who *sees* takes off his shoes,
> The rest sit round and pluck blackberries.[8]

Psalm-shaped people take time to see what God has done in nature. Psalm-shaped people listen for the wind and birds and yes, even the gurgle of babies. For humans also are part of God's stunning creation. Psalm-shaped people worship before the wonder of God in nature.

PSALM-SHAPED PEOPLE ALSO AFFIRM OUR STEWARDSHIP FOR THIS WONDERFUL WORLD GOD CREATED.

We remember that humans were put in the Garden of Eden to take care of it, not just to use up its wealth. The "dominion" of the Genesis commission to Adam and Eve is about stewardship and caring, not neglect or misuse (Gen. 1:19; 2:15). Psalm-shaped people grieve and lament over the spoiling of

8. Elizabeth Barrett Browning, *Aurora Leigh*, 7.821–24.

nature by oil spills, strip mining, and deforestation. Psalm-shaped people plant trees because we are partners with God in caring for the "good" creation. Psalm-shaped people inquire of legislation, both local and national, as to whether it safeguards creation concerns. These are not partisan political issues. These are psalm-shaped issues. Could it be that a psalm-shaped life even impacts our politics?

Pray and sing nature psalms in the quiet of morning and splendor of sunset.

Together with fellow believers, sing hymns and contemporary praise songs that incorporate this psalm-shaped nature vision.

Pray and sing nature psalms rather than being merely consumers of God's created beauty.

Let nature psalms shape our lives by giving us a fresh vision of who God is, and a voice with language to celebrate God's creativity.

> O Lord, how manifold are your works!
> In wisdom you have made them,
> The earth is full of your creatures. . . .
> When you send forth your Spirit, they are created;
> And you renew the face of the earth. (Ps. 104:24, 30)

PRAYING FROM PSALM 19

At Palisades Retreat Center overlooking Puget Sound

God of beauty, order and creativity, I look out on sea and sky today and celebrate what they say and sing about you.

The panorama before me turns mind and heart to your glory.

Your creation invites me to bow and be in wonder.

But you also speak in Torah, guidance, precepts, commandments, decrees, ordinances.

Living your way brings not only order but delight.

I desire you and desire your ways, which keep me from being in bondage to hidden faults and public wrongs.

Let my words and inner ponderings please you. That is my heart's desire today.

You, Lord, are my Rock and my Redeemer!

Amen!

4

Psalm-Shaped Storytelling

Our ancestors have told us,
What deeds you performed in their days
in the days of old. (Ps. 44:1)

OUR PERSONAL AND FAMILY STORIES SHAPE
OUR VISION OF OURSELVES AND WHAT IS
IMPORTANT IN OUR LIVES.

DAN ABBOTT and Catherine May, my brother and
his wife, were recently declared "Humanitarians of
the Year" by the Tempe Community Council in Tempe,
Arizona. One of the ways Dan explained his involvement
in immigration issues, among other things, was a story
my mother used to tell about her father. Charlie Koteskey
was an immigrant from the "old country," trying to make
his way with his family to relatives living in Michigan.
Charlie told about how the Koteskey family ran out of
money and became stranded in a Chicago railway station.
These were times, like now, when feelings about immi-
grants to America ran high. But from Charlie's mother's
broken English a fellow traveler discovered the immigrant

family's plight. He decided to do something about it. This stranger passed a hat from one waiting traveler to another so that the Koteskeys could make it all the way to northern Michigan. That family story, told now to the fourth generation, has shaped my brother's calling to be hospitable to those whom the Bible calls "aliens and strangers." Stories and their retelling shape our lives.

One of the defining stories of my pastoral life was about my father's father. Alexander James Abbott, an Englishman, was a Methodist pastor in small town churches in Wisconsin and Minnesota. Soon after arriving at a new pastoral appointment, Alexander found his predecessor had left significant unpaid bills with community businesses. He insisted that the church to which he'd just been appointed pay off these bills *before* they paid his salary. My father and I, both in ministry, have insisted on being "squeaky clean" when it comes to money issues. My ministry values have also been shaped by family story.

These are not just often repeated, long and drawn out stories that "old guys" like me are known to tell. These are the key stories that define who we are and what is important in our lives. These are stories that make us the people we are and give us a sense of mission in life. Like my brother and I, our stories shape who we are and what we consider important in life.

As Eugene Peterson observes, not everyone's life is full of dramatic incidents like David's was. However, "Every day is a story, a morning beginning and evening ending that are boundaries for people who go about their tasks with more or less purpose, go to war, make love, earn a living, scheme and sin and believe. Everything is connected. Meaning is everywhere. The days add up to a life that is a story."[1]

STORIES OF GOD'S FAMILY SHAPE NOT ONLY OUR INDIVIDUAL IDENTITY BUT ALSO HOW WE SEE OURSELVES AS BELIEVING MEMBERS OF THE FAITH COMMUNITY.

These kinds of stories go beyond precepts and principles, do's and don'ts. Family stories become part of our corporate DNA. And it is these stories that we retell Sunday after Sunday in congregational worship and especially in the high holy days of the year, Christmas, Easter, and Pentecost. "Christ has died, Christ is risen, Christ is coming again!" declares the traditional communion ritual. These declarations reaffirm our story in the presence of the gathered congregation.

STORY IS FAST BECOMING THE COMMON THREAD RUNNING THROUGH THE MANY MEDIA OF OUR AGE.

According to Gerard Kelly, "The good news for the Christian faith community is that much of the Bible was story before it was anything else—and that the founder of the faith was without doubt one of history's best storytellers. Christian Scripture is rich with living, colorful, multilayered stories to fund our culture's imagination."[2]

---

1. Peterson, *Answering God*, 47.
2. Kelly, *Retrofuture*, 101.

Storytelling preacher and seminary professor Calvin Miller used to picture graduates leaving seminary either with "a tambourine and a portfolio of choruses" or "a notebook and an interlinear Bible." "Some," writes Miller, "would publish joy, others information. Some would tell stories, others would preach fearsome precepts." Of course, Miller encourages seminarians not to be either a precept or a storytelling preacher. "Storytelling preaching is right brain. It is kept in line by the left brain."[3]

But in many churches, particular in many Bible-believing, evangelical churches, it tends to be either one or the other. It is often storytelling *or* Bible analysis. Sometimes we forget that Jesus preached what we call "the Sermon on the Mount" *and* told parables.

IN PSALMS, THE EVENTS OF THE COMMUNITY'S STORY WERE THE CONTEXT IN WHICH GOD'S PEOPLE CAME TO KNOW THEIR GOD.

Long before Jesus was telling the stories we call parables, the people of ancient Israel told the stories of what God had done for them. And as ancient people did, they often retold their story in song. Psalms 78 and 105, for example, celebrate the story of God's people in great detail.

Listen in as the psalmist's prayer collects the story of his people and offers it back to God.

> We have heard with our ears, O God,
> Our ancestors have told us,
> What deeds you performed in their days in the days
> of old:

3. Miller, *Spirit, Word, and Story*, 157.

> You with your own hand drove out the nations,
> but them [our ancestors] you planted. (Ps. 44:1–2)

Reflecting on what God had done in his people's story moved this psalmist to call on God in a time of current distress. "Rouse yourself! Why do you sleep, O Lord? Awake, do not cast us off forever! Why do you hide your face? Why do you forget our affliction and oppression?" (Ps. 44:23–24).

The Psalms' storytelling reflected on their people's story especially in:

- the story of the exodus, for example, in Psalm 77:15–20;

- the story of establishing David's dynasty, for example, in Psalm 89:3–4;

- the story of exile and return from exile, as in Psalms 126 and 137.

THE PSALMS' STORYTELLING REFLECTED NOT ONLY ON THE FAITH COMMUNITY STORY BUT ALSO ON PERSONAL STORIES OF SUFFERING, DELIVERANCE, AND HEALING.

Hope for the future rested on what God had done in the past. The Psalmists' own life stories shaped the character of their prayers. Notice some of the titles offered as preludes to several psalms. Imagine how events in these poets' lives shaped their vision of God and their voice to God.

- "A Psalm of David when he fled from his son Absalom" (Ps. 3). Imagine the angst of having your own son rebel against you, ousting you from your palace and capital city!

- "A Psalm of David the servant of the Lord, who addressed the word of this song to the Lord on the day when the Lord delivered him from the hand of all his enemies, and from the hand of Saul." (Ps. 18)

- "A Maskil of David, when Doeg the Edomite came to Saul and said to him, 'David has come to the house of Ahimelech.'" (Ps. 52; read about this in 1 Sam. 21)

- "A Psalm of David when the prophet Nathan came to him, after he had gone in to Bathsheba." (Ps. 51)

How does our experience of God in the midst of life's troubles, even in the midst of our sin (as in the intensely penitential tones of Psalm 51), shape our lives? Do we turn toward God in lament, in hope, and in praise by reliving the stories of these times? Listen as one psalm reflects on the anguish of a difficult time:

> I cry aloud to God,
> aloud to God, that he may hear me.
> In the day of my trouble I seek the Lord;
> in the night my hand is stretched out without wearying;
> my soul refuses to be comforted.
> I think of God, and I moan;
> I meditate, and my spirit faints. (Ps. 77:1–3)

The psalmist goes on to pepper God with intense questions:

> Will the Lord spurn for ever,
> And never again be favorable?
> Has his steadfast love ceased for ever?

> Are his promises at an end for all time?
> Has God forgotten to be gracious?
> Has he in anger shut up his compassion? (Ps. 77:7–9)

But in the midst of his difficulty and honest lament the psalmist calls to mind the story of what God had done for God's people. "I will call to mind the deeds of the Lord; I will remember your wonders of old. I will meditate on all your work, and muse on your mighty deeds" (Ps. 77:11–12).

Notice the "calling to mind," the remembering, meditating, and musing on the story of God's great acts. It was out of remembering the story within which God's people lived out their lives that the ancient poet found hope.

> Your way, O God, is holy.
> What god is so great as our God?
> You are the God who works wonders;
> you have displayed your might among the peoples.
> With your strong arm you redeemed your people,
> the descendants of Jacob and Joseph. (Ps. 77:13–15)

Paul Warren writes, "When we bring the insights of faith to bear upon the past, we discover the wondrous works of God and are led to praise him."[4] When our vision of God is shaped by our own story and that of our faith community, we turn to God with the voice of hope even in the midst of adversity. What we do in congregational worship is to retell our story of what God has done for us in Jesus.

Starbucks has urged us, "Take comfort in rituals." Of course, Starbucks wants us to read that motto and think of regular rituals involving hot drinks and visits to its stores. "Will you have your regular today?" baristas sometimes ask

4. Warren, *Hymnbook of the Ages*, 20.

their customers. Good baristas know what regular customers order. But thinking beyond Starbucks, what about rituals that involve the retelling of our great story? Do we "take
comfort" (*cum-forte*, or "take strength") from faith rituals
such as the Lord's Supper, which most basically retell the
story of what God has done for us in Jesus? What we do in
congregational worship is to retell our story. What we do in
the celebration of the Lord's Supper is to reenact the story
which shapes who we are and what we do. Story Psalms can
help us "take comfort" in this ritual.

As a pastor I urge Sunday worshipers who are in
the midst any kind of difficulty to remember what God
had done in their lives. If they can't connect with a hope-
inspiring story of their own, I urge them to hang on to the
community's story, which is retold in worship. Thus Sunday
worship should not always be triumphal and happy. In a
subsequent chapter we will reflect on the importance of
learning to lament in worship. Honest lament issuing in
hope and trust-inspiring retelling of the community's story
provides troubled people with the great story to hang on to
even if their own experience of it is tenuous.

The great story of what God has done needs to be repeated, told, and retold. Again and again we need to reaffirm, "The Lord's steadfast love endures forever." Listen for
the repetition in selections from the monumental Psalm 136:

> O give thanks to the Lord, for he is good,
> For his steadfast love endures forever.
> O give thanks to the God of gods,
> For his steadfast love endures forever.
> O give thanks to the Lord of lords,
> For his steadfast love endures forever. (Ps. 136:1–3)

Through stanza after stanza this marathon psalm retells the stories of creation, exodus, and entrance into the Promised Land, all the while reiterating, "For his steadfast love endures forever."

The story of God's ancient people who gave us the Psalms is the story of a people and their God. This God was characterized by steadfast, covenant, faithful love—love that "endures forever." And that is our God also. The God who supremely revealed himself in Jesus loved even followers who left him in the lurch, who betrayed and denied him. Jesus was lovingly faithful to his friends to the point of death. This is our Good News story! We need to tell and retell it for ourselves and for the sake of the community.

OUR STORY GUIDES IN HOW TO LIVE.

Paul wrote to Corinthian believers about the experience of Israel in the wilderness. After referencing this well-known story, the apostle adds, "Now these things occurred as examples for us, so that we might not desire evil as they did. . . . These things happened to them to serve as an example and they were written down to instruct us, on whom the ends of the ages have come" (1 Cor. 10:1–11).

In other words, let the community's story of belief and unbelief instruct our lives. Let us learn who we are and how we should live by retelling our great story.

HERE ARE QUESTIONS I INVITE US TO ASK OURSELVES ABOUT OUR STORY.

- How are we integrating our personal story with the great story of what God has done for us, especially in Jesus? How do we connect our own story with this great story?

- How do we, or how should we, allow the faith community's storytelling to shape our lives?

- How do we, or how should we, use storytelling in community worship? One of the great benefits of following the church year in worship is the retelling of the great story of Jesus, beginning with Advent through Christmas and Epiphany, continuing through Lent, Holy Week, and Easter, and moving on to Pentecost and Ascension. Is Christian worship really complete without storytelling?

Let storytelling psalms shape our lives as we relive with them what God has done for God's people in history and what God has done for us today.

PRAYING FROM PSALM 18

You, Lord, are my rock, fortress, deliverer, and refuge in time of distress and trouble.

I call upon you in praise for you are worthy.
I also call upon you to deal with what is troubling me.
I cry out for help in my distress.

And I watch how you respond to little me and to my cry for help.

I stand amazed at how you move heaven and earth to deliver and support and set me again in a wide-open space.

You light up my dark places and defeat what distresses me.

You boost me over the wall that has hemmed me in.

That's your way, God. You are a shield for all who take refuge in you!

So I bless you and extol you.

I sing praises to you, living, loving God!

Amen!

PRAYING FROM PSALM 126

Great and gracious God, along with your ancient people I want to affirm that you have done "great things for us."

And I do rejoice in the great story of your grace and goodness in my life and my family.

But I also rejoice in what you have done for the wider people of faith.

Thank you for liberation from Egypt and return from exile.

Thank you for what you have done!

But Lord, there's more that I need.

There is ongoing renewal that I need.

I need to be flooded with your Spirit, living water flowing through me. I want to be "like the watercourses in the Negeb."

Though I sow in tears now, I believe I will reap with shouts of joy.

And I trust you for ongoing renewal in my life because of the great things you have done.

And I rejoice!

Amen!

5

Psalm-Shaped Praise

> Make a joyful noise to God, all the earth;
> Sing the glory of his name;
> Give to him glorious praise. (Ps. 66:1)

> O my strength, I will sing praises to you,
> For you, O God, are my fortress,
> The God who shows me steadfast love. (Ps. 59:17)

S EVERAL OF this year's viral YouTube videos featured seemingly spontaneous, but actually highly orchestrated eruptions of the Hallelujah Chorus in crowded public places. One was in a Macy's and included the store's great pipe organ. The other was in a nondescript food court where, against the backdrop of Arby's and other fast-food places, skilled singers stood or even leaped onto tables and sang this great paean of praise.

> For the Lord God omnipotent reigneth!
> King of Kings and Lord of Lords!
> Hallelujah!

WHEN WE THINK OF PSALMS WE MOST OFTEN THINK PRAISE.

And it is right that we should do so. The very name for Psalms in the Hebrew Bible (*tehillim*) means "Praise be to Yahweh!"

We love to use "calls to praise and worship" from Psalms. Depending on our denomination or the character of our congregation, worship services may be punctuated with exclamations of "Praise the Lord!" Prayers by individuals often include litanies of praises. "We praise you Lord for . . ." Music leaders in many churches are called "praise teams."

BUT WHAT DOES IT MEAN TO PRAISE GOD? AND WHAT WOULD PSALM-SHAPED PRAISES LOOK LIKE?

Part of the Advent-Christmas season for my wife and me is attending not just a rendition of the Hallelujah Chorus but an uncut presentation of Handel's "Messiah." Of course, we enjoy the first section with its retelling of the Christmas story. But we continue on into the second section's somber portrayal of Jesus's crucifixion and the "raging of the heathen" against the Lord. But it is this darker section, not the brighter Christmas story, that concludes with the stunning Hallelujah Chorus. Agnostic or believer, in Macy's, a food court, or concert hall, listeners are caught up in this eruption of praise. But we stick with the music until the final magnificent "Worthy is the Lamb" leading into the concluding "Amen" chorus. This climax to "Messiah" includes a section in which a quiet line of music by violins in unison is answered by the full-throated chorus of "Amen." Praise can be like that. Sometimes it's a single line of music played by unison violins—quiet, contemplative, meditative. Sometimes it's a great, full-throated chorus lifting us almost to heaven. At the wonderful church I was privileged to pastor for twenty-eight years, we began Easter Sunday morning in quiet wonder with various voices, then the whole congregation singing, "Were you there . . . when they crucified my Lord . . . when He rose up from the dead?" But quiet praise moved to the great Easter Greeting: "The Lord is risen! He is risen indeed!" Then, we erupted into the great Easter hymn "Christ the Lord Is Risen Today" accompanied by bells church members knew to bring that Sunday. We closed the Easter morning sanctuary service by a sing-a-long "Hallelujah Chorus." Easter demands both quiet and celebrative praise. We experience both those kinds of praises in the Psalms.

In his excellent little book *Reflections on the Psalms*, C. S. Lewis observes, "Praise almost seems to be inner health made audible. Nor does it cease to be so when, through lack of skill, the forms of its expression are very uncouth or even ridiculous. . . . The Psalmists in telling everyone to praise God are doing what all men do when they speak of what they care about. . . . We delight to praise what we enjoy because the praise not merely expresses but completes the enjoyment."[1]

Praise to God expresses deep delight in who God is and what God does. If C. S. Lewis is correct, the expression of our praise is part of and completes our delight in God.

1. Lewis, *Reflections on the Psalms*, 94.

PRAISE IS AN ESSENTIAL PART OF BOTH
PERSONAL AND CORPORATE WORSHIP.

Delight in God through worship is made audible or expressed in our praises. C. S. Lewis again writes, "It is in the process of being worshiped that God communicates His presence to men. It is not of course the only way. But for many people at many times, the 'fair beauty of the Lord' is revealed chiefly or only while they worship Him together."[2]

Delight in God, arising out of the health of our relationship with God and enhancing the health of that relationship, is expressed in praise to God. Praise is thus not some added-on veneer, nor a "Pollyanna positive" perspective on life. Praise is deep-down delight in God. While our praise to God is called for and expected by God, it is not merely a divine demand to which we respond. Praise comes from deep down inside us and is shaped by what we truly believe about God.

Medieval English poet and pastor John Donne spoke of praise as "tuning our instruments," preparing for the real thing we will do forever in God's presence. Go to a symphony concert and you will first be treated to a blowing and bowing and banging by the orchestra. That is not the concert you came to hear. This is rather the tuning of instruments in preparation for the concert. So a praise-shaped life here and now prepares us for the fullest experience of praise we will enjoy in heaven. All the more reason for living a praise-shaped life in the here and now!

2. Ibid., 93.

THANKSGIVING GOES TOGETHER WITH PRAISE.

Offering heartfelt thanks to God for who God is and what God has done is an essential part of praise. Listen to Psalm 50: "Offer to God a sacrifice of thanksgiving. . . . Those who bring thanksgiving as their sacrifice honor me" (Ps. 50:14, 23).

Henri Nouwen has observed, "Without a spirit of gratitude, life flattens out and becomes dull and boring. But when we continue to be surprised by new manifestations of life and continue to praise and thank God and our neighbor, routine and boredom cannot take hold. Then all of life becomes a reason for saying thanks. . . . Gratitude belongs to the core of the life of Jesus and His followers."[3] Praise and thanksgiving go together. A psalm-shaped life is filled with praise and thanks to God!

NOWHERE DO WE LEARN PRAISING BY EXAMPLE MORE THAN IN THE PSALMS.

Nowhere is this central praising core of the believing life highlighted more than in the Psalms. Psalm 33:1 sings, "Praise befits the upright." And from Psalm 65:1, "Praise is due to you, O God, in Zion!" Nowhere is there a more powerful vision of the praiseworthiness of God than in the Psalms. Nowhere is there clearer voice, even words given to us with which to praise our God. Praise God in these psalm fragments:

3. Nouwen, *Lifesigns*, 68.

> Every day I will bless you,
> And praise your name for ever and ever. (Ps. 145:2)

> I will praise the Lord as long as I live.
> I will sing praises to my God all my life long. (Ps. 146:2)

The book of Psalms reaches its climax in an outpouring of praise in the last five psalms sometimes known as "hallelujah psalms." Each of these paeans of praise begins and ends with the exclamation "Hallelujah," usually translated "Praise the Lord!" Psalm 150 crescendos to its climax: "Let everything that breathes praise the Lord! Praise the Lord!" (Ps. 150:6).

The Psalms shape our *vision* of the God we delight in. And the Psalms give us *voice* to express that delight.

AS WE PRAY THE PSALMS, WE PRAISE, BLESS, AND THANK GOD IN AT LEAST TWO ESSENTIAL WAYS.

Narrative Praise

One way is to praise God for what God does. Much of the time our praise is for what God does *for us*. This is often called *narrative praise*. It is narrating or retelling what God has done for us. How many times do we pray, "Oh God, I praise you for all the wonderful things you have done for us, for me?" We used to sing, "Count your blessings, name them one by one, and it will surprise you what the Lord has done."

The Psalms are full of this kind of narrative praise. Listen to Psalm 30:

> I will extol you, O Lord, for you have drawn me up,
> and did not let my foes rejoice over me.
> O Lord my God, I cried to you for help,
> and you have healed me.
> O Lord, you brought up my soul from Sheol,
> restored me to life from among those gone down to the Pit.
> Sing praises to the Lord, O you his faithful ones,
> and give thanks to his holy name.
> For his anger is but for a moment;
> his favor is for a lifetime.
> Weeping may linger for a night,
> But joy comes with the morning. (Ps. 30:1–5)

Listen to another psalm celebrating the "benefits" received from God, the good things God has done for the poet.

> Bless the Lord, O my soul,
> And do not forget all his benefits—
> Who forgives all your iniquity,
> Who heals all your diseases,
> Who redeems your life from the Pit,
> Who crowns you with steadfast love and mercy,
> Who satisfies you with good as long as you live
> so that your youth is renewed like the eagle's.
> (Ps. 103:2–5)

Often, the psalmists begin with an announcement of or call to praise: "I will extol you O Lord" (Ps. 30:1). Or listen to Psalm 34: "I will bless the Lord at all times, his praise shall continually be in my mouth" (Ps. 34:1). The beginning of Psalm 107 is heard periodically in the Psalter: "O give thanks to the Lord, for he is good, for his steadfast love endures forever" (Ps. 107:1).

After the opening announcement or call to praise, there is a retelling of God's acts in response to the psalmist's cry for help. Narrative praise often includes a "life-situation stimulus," a problem facing the psalmist. The implication of Psalm 30 is that the psalmist had been sick to the point of death. But God had delivered him from death. "You did not let my foes rejoice over me. . . . You have healed me. . . . O Lord, you . . . restored me to life from among those gone down to the Pit" (Ps. 30:1–3).

The Psalm 30 narrative of God's deeds continues with a description of the crisis, the rescue, and the offering of praise:

> You have turned my mourning into dancing;
> You have taken off my sackcloth
> And clothed me with joy,
> So that my soul may praise you and not be silent.
> O Lord my God, I will give thanks to you forever.
> (Ps. 30:11–12)

We love these psalms of narrative praise. We love to quote them when we celebrate the wonderful things God has done for us. We rightly use the language of these psalms to express praise for what God has done for us. We love to "count our blessings, name them one by one." But what happens when things don't seem so wonderful? What about when "blessings" seem few and far between? What about when our lives are filled with difficulty? Can we praise God even then?

Descriptive Praise

When difficulty and hard times fill the horizons of our lives, we turn from narrative praise to *descriptive praise*. We praise God for who God is in God's very nature. We describe the character and nature of God in our praise. Listen to the familiar praises of Psalm 100. The poet urges us to praise God: "Make a joyful noise to the Lord, all the earth. Worship the Lord with gladness. . . . Enter his gates with thanksgiving" (Ps. 100:1–2, 4).

But when the reason for this outpouring of praise is given it is not in what God has done for us. The reason for praise is in the very character of God. "Know that the Lord is God, it is he that made us, and we are his. . . . The Lord is good; his steadfast love endures forever, and his faithfulness to all generations" (Ps. 100:3, 5).

Reading and praying the Psalms redirects our vision to God's "steadfast love and faithfulness." Reading and praying the Psalms gives us voice, even words and phrases to praise God for his "steadfast love and faithfulness." "It is good to give thanks to the Lord, to sing praises to your name, O Most High, to declare your steadfast love in the morning, and your faithfulness by night" (Ps. 92:1).

Are there not times when we need to praise God for who God is even though we cannot see anything good in our lives? Are there not times when there is nothing that seems good in our circumstances, but we hang on to the realities that God's love is steadfast and God is faithful? Are there not times when the best way to reach out to God is to call our divine friend by the names given in the Psalms? Listen to the piled up images in Psalm 144's address to God:

"My rock, and my fortress, my stronghold and my deliverer, my shield, in whom I take refuge" (Ps. 144:2).

Eugene Peterson's *The Message* begins to paraphrase those ancient Middle Eastern word pictures for us: "He's the bedrock on which I stand, the castle in which I live, my rescuing knight, the high crag where I run for dear life, while he lays my enemies low." This is descriptive praise—praising God for who God is even in the midst of difficulty.

"God is good!" I once heard pastors in Malawi declare. And the loud and clear response from the congregations was, "All the time." I also hear that affirmation periodically in affluent American congregations. But in the extreme poverty of these African brothers and sisters, they know that even when things are very, very hard, God is still good. And they offer praise by describing the character of God.

In a psalm-like passage from the short but powerful prophecy of Habakkuk, the poet describes agricultural catastrophe:

> Though the fig tree does not blossom
> And no fruit is on the vines,
> Though the produce of the olive fail,
> And the fields yield no food,
> Though the flock is cut off from the fold,
> And there is no herd in the stalls . . . (Hab. 3:17)

Translate that into contemporary, Western terms:

> Though the stock market has nose-dived,
> And my IRAs are worth half what they once were,
> Though I've had a diagnosis of cancer and my future is
> filled with chemotherapy,

> Though I've lost my job and there are no employment prospects on the horizon of my life . . .

The psalm-like prophecy reaches its climax with what someone has called "the invincible *yet*."

> Yet I will rejoice in the Lord,
> I will exult in the God of my salvation.
> God, the Lord, is my strength. (Hab. 3:18–19)

A contemporary praise song is almost psalm-like in its expression of praise for who God is. After revisiting times of trial and doubt, the songwriter echoes the refrain, "I will praise Him still."

> I will praise Him *still*!
> Even when the narrative of my life looks bleak . . .

Even when my sky is clouded with discouragement, even depression.

> Even when the diagnosis *is* cancer,
> I will praise Him still!

PSALM-SHAPED SPIRITUALITY DOES NOT PRAISE GOD FOR THE HARD THINGS OF LIFE BUT IN THE MIDST OF THE HARD THINGS OF LIFE.

We are not called to pray, "Hallelujah, I've got cancer!" Psalm-shaped spirituality realistically praises God for who God is in the midst of life's adversity. That distinction avoids denial of reality when life is full of trouble. That distinction shapes a way of life that faces up to hard times and our natural feelings about hard times, but then redirects our attention to who God is in the midst of our trouble.

An aged, asthma-afflicted saint could be heard gasping between painful wheezing breaths, "Praise the Lord! Hallelujah! Glory to God!" A younger family member asked, "Grandma, what do you have to praise the Lord for? Why are you using your strength like this?" The old saint smiled and said, "I praise God for who God is, not for what comes into my life. It brings peace to my heart and makes the suffering easier to bear." That's a psalm-shaped life! Listen once more to the psalmist's descriptive praise: "My flesh and my heart may fail, but God is the strength [Hebrew, "rock"] of my heart and my portion forever" (Ps. 73:26).

The Psalms shape our lives as we exercise both narrative praise and descriptive praise. Sometimes we call this subjective and objective praise. Subjective praise celebrates God in the blessings of my experience. Objective praise celebrates God objectively, that is, as we know God to be, in God's very self. Both are important for a healthy spiritual formation.

The Psalmist declares, "My praise is continually of you" (Ps. 71:6). A psalm-shaped life is a praise-dominated life—often narrative praise, celebrating the wonderful things God has done, but sometimes descriptive praise, offering praise to God for who God is.

BUT HOW DO WE GET THERE? HOW DO WE INCREASINGLY OPEN OURSELVES TO THE PRAISE-SHAPING IMPACT OF THE PSALMS?

- Obviously, *we swim daily in the Psalms*. We let their vision of God shape the way we look at and interact with our God. We allow them to give voice both to subjective and objective praise.

- We also recognize that *psalm-shaped praise is based in memory*, the memory of what God has done. And if our own memory feels inadequate, we may have to hitchhike on fellow believers' memories and the memory of the community's story. "I will call to mind the deeds of the Lord, I will remember your wonders of old, I will meditate on all your work, and muse on your mighty deeds" (Ps. 77:11–12).

- Psalm-shaped praise is also based in choice. It is, "I *will* praise the Lord!" That is why the psalms fervently exhort us to praise. It would be unreasonable to exhort us to something that is not subject to our choice. We can praise God when we feel like it and when we don't feel like it if that is what we choose to do. Praise is a choice based not on circumstances, but a choice made regardless of circumstances.

Have we recently chosen to praise God even when we didn't feel like it?

PSALM-SHAPED PRAISE IS BOTH INDIVIDUAL AND CORPORATE.

Are there hymns, praise songs, snatches of psalms that we use off and on all day long? Can we remember this past Sunday's songs on Monday and Friday? In the midst of an individualistic, consumer-based culture that has encroached on how we think of congregational worship, we hear the corrective of the Psalms. We praise God together as the community gathers for worship! We worship together partly to remind ourselves and to remind each other that ours is to be a praise-dominated life.

THIS KIND OF SPIRITUAL FORMATION IS ALSO VITAL IN OUR RELATIONSHIPS WITH ONE ANOTHER.

A praise-shaped life is important as we take delight in God individually and together. But what would happen to the quality and tone of our relationships if our lives were shaped and dominated by praise? We would surely be active in building each other, encouraging each other, affirming one another. We would surely look for things to take delight in rather than for things to dismiss or condemn. Praise-shaped lives lead to praise-shaped relationships. A praise-shaped life leads to a praise-shaped community.

Let praise psalms shape our lives as we return to them again and again to celebrate what God has done for us and who we believe God is, even in the midst of adversity.

PRAYING FROM PSALM 27

O God, my light, my salvation, my stronghold, I thank you that I can come to you without being afraid.

Your face, Lord, do I seek.

I want to behold you in all your beauty.

But most of all today I want to celebrate your great goodness in the midst of life.

Despite appearances and opinions to the contrary, I believe you are good, always good, with your goodness ultimately revealed in Jesus.

In your goodness, I take heart.

In your goodness, I rest and wait and trust.

I believe that I shall see the goodness of the Lord in the land of the living.

Amen!

PRAYING FROM PSALM 34

Lord, I want to bless you not just when I feel like it or when I feel good about life.

I want to bless you at all times, praise continually in my heart and mouth.

I want to magnify and exalt your name with others who believe in you.

I want to taste and see that you are good, always good.

I want to live in the light of your goodness.

I want to be aware of and respond to your nearness, even, or especially, in times when I feel my own brokenness.

I confess that when I am conscious of my human brokenness, I sometimes find it all too easy to be numb to your presence.

Help me even in those times to turn toward you and respond to your face that is always turned toward me.

Amen!

6

Psalm-Shaped Lament

I am weary with my moaning;
Every night I flood my bed with tears;
I drench my couch with my weeping. (Ps. 6:6)

O Lord, I cry out to you;
In the morning my prayer comes before you.
O Lord, why do you cast me off?
Why do you hide your face from me? (Ps. 88:13–14)

I LED a mission team to Rwanda a few years after the tragic genocide there. Painful memories were still fresh and tender. A bullet-ridden vehicle remained in a church compound. At a pastors' gathering I gently tried to probe their responses to what happened. "Did you use the psalms of lament to express your feelings?" I asked. The reaction was negative. I got the impression they thought godly people, especially pastors, should not pray to God like that.

In fact there is powerful precedent in Scripture for prayers of lament. In addition to the psalms of lament, listen for lament in the Old Testament prophets and in the book of Lamentations. Listen to Naomi's lament in the book of Ruth:

Call me no longer Naomi, call me Mara,
For the Almighty has dealt bitterly with me.
I went away full, but the Lord has brought me back
empty;
Why call me Naomi when the Lord has dealt harshly
with me,
And the Almighty has brought calamity upon me?
(Ruth 1:20–21)

According to Matthew's Gospel, in the tragic massacre of little children after Jesus's birth and the lament of bereaved mothers was the fulfillment of Jeremiah's prophecy: "A voice was heard in Ramah, wailing and loud lamentation, Rachel weeping for her children; she refused to be consoled, because they are no more" (2:18). There is also the powerful precedent of Jesus on the cross, giving voice to his lament in the words of Psalm 22: "My God, my God, why have you forsaken me?" (Matt. 26:46)

How else would God's ancient people deal with seventh-century BC defeat and exile? How else would one deal with cruel rulers like Herod at the time of Jesus's birth? How else would one deal with the cross, where Jesus felt forsaken by his God?

Why shouldn't Rwandans lament their tragedy to God? How else would one honestly and openly deal in prayer with genocide?

How else would one deal with the searing images of 9/11, with horrific oil spills in the Gulf of Mexico, with earthquakes, hurricanes, and epidemics in already impoverished Haiti, followed the next year by earthquakes, tsunamis, and nuclear tragedy in Japan? How else should one deal with tragic mass shootings by deranged people, with ongoing deaths of Americans and civilians in Iraq and Afghanistan, with the cruel killing of citizens in North Africa demonstrating for freedom?

How else should one deal with the weight of sin and personal failure? How else would one respond to betrayal of trust by a close friend or a loved one? How else should one respond to a flood of personal adversity?

LAMENT IS SORROW POURED OUT TO GOD.

"Praise and lament are the two basic melodies which, like echoes, accompany God's actions on this long path of history. . . . Lament is sorrow poured out to God," writes Old Testament scholar Claus Westermann. Laments accompany the entire path of God's people, including laments of the wilderness wanderers; Moses, the lonely intermediary between the people and God; Elijah and other prophets, especially Jeremiah; laments of exiles over their displacement to Babylon; and Jesus's own tearful lament over Jerusalem and his cry of dereliction from the cross. In the Psalms, these laments, says Westermann, "are developed into mighty fugues and variations . . . different from the familiar polarity of thanksgiving and petition in our modern prayers."[1]

The most frequent category of Psalms, by some estimates as high as seventy percent, is lament. Lament is the outpouring of human feeling to God in the midst of difficulty, questions, and low feelings. Lament is this outpouring of feeling in the course of a life's journey that also includes praise and thanks—especially descriptive praise (for who God is). Sometimes our journey passes through

1. Westermann, *Psalms*, 11.

times of questioning, anger, sorrow, even haughty self-justification—all of which are openly expressed to God. But the believer's journey need not become stuck at these stages. Instead we may move through them toward praise to God. At all stages of the journey, the believer's heart is open to God.

When David was in distress, he lamented. David faced loss, disappointment, and death head-on with his responses to adversity poured out before God. But David did not usually become bogged down or stuck in lament. Lament was part of the journey, part of his story faced honestly in God's presence.

"When he was in the cave. A Prayer" is the heading of Psalm 142. David, then a refugee from King Saul, cries out to God, "With my voice I cry to the Lord; with my voice I make supplication to the Lord, I pour out my complaint before him; I tell my trouble before him" (Ps. 142:1–2).

This psalmist's journey does not move to fully voiced praise as in some psalms. However, David moves through his outpouring of complaint and trouble to conclude with trust in God. "Bring me out of prison, so that I may give thanks to your name. The righteous will surround me, for you will deal bountifully with me" (Ps. 142:7).

The Psalms illustrate *community lament*, a national crisis brought before God. Listen to Psalm 80, "A Psalm of Asaph," probably in response to the defeat of Judah and the exile to Babylon.

> O Lord God of Hosts, how long will you be angry with your people's prayers?
> You have fed them with the bread of tears
> And given them tears to drink in full measure.

> You make us the scorn of our neighbors;
> Our enemies laugh among themselves. (Ps. 80:4–6)

In what kinds of contemporary settings might a psalm like this give voice to a community of believers' cries?

"Oh Lord, we cry out to you in horror over the shooting rampage in Arizona!"

"Oh Lord, we cry out to you in sadness over those who suffer the aftermath of earthquakes, tsunamis, and nuclear disaster!"

"Oh Lord, we grieve over the money-hungry greed of people whose only thought seems to be of themselves and not of the poor around them!"

"Oh Lord, we lament continuing warfare in the Middle East!"

Often the best corporate response to a week's news is not comment but community lament.

The *individual lament*, most common of the laments, is individual trouble brought before God. Psalm 13 is a classic individual lament. Follow the journey of the psalmist's outpouring of feeling to God.

There is an *invocation* or *opening*, which, in some laments, is combined with a plea for help. "How long, O Lord? Will you forget me forever? How long will you hide your face from me?" (Ps. 13:1).

There is *complaint* poured out honestly to God. Sometimes complaint involves personal issues. Sometimes it involves others' actions. Sometimes the complaint is about how God seems to be treating the psalmist. Listen to the complaints of Psalm 13: "How long must I bear pain in my soul, and have sorrow in my heart all day long? How long shall my enemy be exalted over me?" (Ps. 13:2).

In another psalm, the poet specifically addresses his complaint to how God seems to be responding or not responding: "Why, O Lord, do you stand far off? Why do you hide yourself in times of trouble?" (Ps. 10:1).

What often follows in psalms of lament is *a list of petitions* wrung from the anguished heart of the psalmist.

> Consider and answer me, O Lord my God!
> Give light to my eyes, or I will sleep the sleep of death,
> and my enemy will say, "I have prevailed,"
> my foes will rejoice because I am shaken? (Ps. 13:3–4)

In some psalms, there are *curses on enemies*. We will reflect on them in a moment. These are what we call "psalms of imprecation" (see, for example, Ps. 109:8–9). In some psalms the poet *confesses sin or asserts innocence* (26:3–6; 51:3–4). We will consider the penitential psalms as a kind of lament in a moment. But in Psalm 13, as in most psalms of lament, the psalmist works through the outpouring of troubled feelings to an *expression of praise and trust in God*. "But I trusted in your steadfast love; my heart shall rejoice in your salvation. I will sing to the Lord, because he has dealt bountifully with me" (Ps. 13:5–6).

Often praise and trust includes an expression of confidence in God's response. "Cast your burden on the Lord, and He will sustain you; He will never permit the righteous to be moved" (Ps. 55:22). And, "Trust in him at all times, O people; pour out your heart before him; God is a refuge for us" (Ps. 62:8).

HOW IMPORTANT THIS KIND OF PRAYING IS TO OUR HEALTH!

Philip Yancey calls this kind of psalm "soul therapy." Yancey, who discovered for himself the shaping power of the Psalms, observes, "From Psalms I have learned that I can rightfully bring to God *whatever* I feel about him. I need not paper over my failures and try to clean up my own rottenness; far better to bring those weaknesses to god, who alone has the power to heal." Again and again, says Yancey, he has been amazed "by the spiritual wholeness of the Hebrew poets, who sought to include God in every area of life by bring to God every emotion experienced in daily activity. One need not 'dress up' or 'put on a face' to meet God. There are no walled-off areas; God can be trusted with reality."[2]

How does lament give vision and voice to our prayers? Are we afraid to lament like the psalmists did to God? Or would we prefer to visit a psychiatrist? We may need to do both. But I wonder if a life shaped by the outpouring of all kinds of feelings to God would not foster emotional and even physical health.

Do we think that our prayers in time of trouble need to be edited with our wrenching and angry reactions filtered out? Eugene Peterson writes in the introduction to the Psalms in *The Message*, "We suppose that there must be an 'insider' language that must be acquired before God takes us seriously in our prayer. There is not. Prayer is elemental, not advanced language. It is the means by which our language becomes honest, true, and personal in response to

2. Yancey, *Bible Jesus Read*, 123.

God. It is the means by which we get everything in our lives out in the open before God."[3]

It is this kind of gut-wrenching openness we experience with the psalms of lament. In them, we find no pat answers to life's troubling questions. In them we experience believers in anguish, like many today, but believers who are waiting on God in their anguish.

Not so long ago, a member of our family was in intensive care. I remember walking up and down the hospital stairwell rather than taking the painfully slow elevator. My heart was crying out to God. But all that would come was "Oh God! Oh God!" That was basic lament. And it led to more complete cries to the One who did deliver from death and restore to health.

Have we ever prayed something like this?

"God, I'm so upset that you have not answered my prayers for much needed employment!"

"God, why do I have to go through another round of chemotherapy?"

"Lord, why does it feel like you are so far away, your presence seemingly blotted out by a dark cloud?"

"Good God, bring justice to bear against those who misuse the poor and steal from other people's pension plans! Let them face the consequences for their misdeeds!"

Yes, Psalms are "soul therapy." Even, or especially, psalms of lament give us voice to pour out our inner feelings to God. And they shape our life with God, which includes bringing all our experiences honestly and openly to God.

3. Peterson, *Message*, 910.

BUT WHAT DO WE DO WITH ANGRY, BITTER, EVEN CURSING PSALMS?

In a mid-week local church class on the Psalms, we agreed that this kind of psalm, "imprecatory psalms" as we sometimes call them, is really only for adults. They are not good material for children's stories!

Are these kinds of psalms appropriate "righteous indignation" over evil?

Are imprecatory psalms expressive of spiritual immaturity to be corrected by a New Testament perspective?

Or are these angry psalms honest, open prayers, alternatives to personal revenge and to denying or suppressing our feelings?

Some of us are embarrassed over the imprecatory psalms. But why should these honest outpourings to a personal God, who feels along with us in our pain, cause us to blush? Why not acknowledge that is really the way we sometimes feel?

Eugene Peterson urges us to pray even our hate. "We put on our 'Sunday best' in our prayers. But when we pray the prayers of God's people, the Psalms, we find that will not do. We must pray who we actually are, not who we think we should be. Here [Ps. 137] is a prayer that brings out not the best but the worst in us: vile, venomous, vicious hate. Can God handle our hate?"[4]

Miroslav Volf, a Croatian who taught theology in his native land during the war in former Yugoslavia, learned to identify very personally with these cursing psalms. Volf writes,

4. Peterson, *Living the Message*, 282.

> For the followers of the crucified Messiah, the
> main message of the imprecatory psalms is
> this: rage belongs before God. . . . By placing
> unattended rage before God we place both our
> unjust enemy and our own vengeful self face to
> face with a God who loves and does justice. . . .
> Hidden in the dark chambers of our hearts . . .
> hate grows and seeks to infest everything with its
> hellish will to exclusion. In the light of the justice
> and love of God, however, hate recedes and the
> seed is planted for the miracle of forgiveness."[5]

How do we deal with injustice and evil? Should we
deny their existence? Should we try to redress injustice ourselves? Or should we offer up our feelings about injustice
and evil, unvarnished, unedited, to God, who seems to be
able to accept the full gamut of human feelings? How much
better to tell God how much you think your enemies should
be struck down than to do it yourself!

Eugene Peterson wisely observes, "Embarrassed by
the ugliness and fearful of the murderous, we commonly
neither admit or pray our hate; we deny it and suppress it.
But if it is not admitted it can quickly and easily metamor-
phose into the evil that provokes it; and if it is not prayed
we have lost an essential insight and energy in doing battle
with evil."[6]

"God," says Yancey, "has a high threshold of tolerance
for what is appropriate to say in a prayer. God can 'handle'
my unsuppressed rage."[7] When complaint and rage is what

5. Quoted in Yancey, *Bible Jesus Read*, 138.

6. Peterson, *Answering God*, 98.

7. Yancey, *Bible Jesus Read*, 139.

we honestly feel at a particular stage of our journey, that is what we should pour out to God. No, it is not healthy to become stuck at that stage in the journey. It is healthy to move through it honestly and openly, but not to stay in the lament mode.

WHAT ABOUT LAMENT OVER OUR SINS?

Seven psalms are traditionally known as "penitential" (6, 32, 38, 51, 102, 130, 143). Those that have most shaped believers' understanding of sin and how to respond to it are Psalms 32 and 51. In these psalms, lament is not just sad or guilty feelings about what we have done. Penitential lament is most basically living truthfully regarding our failures. "You desire truth in the inward being, therefore teach me wisdom in my secret heart" (Ps. 51:6). And, "While I kept silence [about sin], my body wasted away. . . . Then I acknowledged my sin to you and I did not hide my iniquity" (Ps. 32:3–5).

Sin at its core is an offense against a relationship, relationship primarily with God, but also with others against whom we have sinned. Penitential lament is facing my offense against my relationship with God truthfully, that is, with confession. Confession is fundamentally truthfulness about myself and about what I have done with God. "Against you, you alone, have I sinned, and done what is evil in your sight" (Ps. 51:4).

Penitential lament involves repentance, a change in direction in reference to our divine friend that results in a change in direction in the specifics of our lives. After deciding to live truthfully about his sin, the author of Psalm 32 hears from God about how he should live. "I will instruct you and teach you the way you should go; I will counsel you with my eye upon you" (Ps. 32:8).

Some churches have a weekly prayer of confession incorporated into congregational worship. While valuable, this does not substitute for regular truth-telling about what we have done and not done. Penitential psalms are often read during the season of Lent. But in this penitential season, these psalms are symbolic of our ongoing need for regular lament over our relational failures with our divine friend.

It is spirit-shaping for believers to "lament" sin. It is spirit-shaping for us to speak truthfully to God and to one another about our failures. It is spirit-shaping on a community-wide basis for penitence to be part of corporate worship. It is health-giving for members of a congregation to pray together and with heartfelt sincerity:

> Create in me a clean heart, O God
> And put a new and right spirit within me. . . .
> Restore to me the joy of your salvation,
> And sustain me in a willing spirit.
> Then I [we] will teach transgressors your ways,
> And sinners will return to you. (Ps. 51:10–13)

What would it take for us to allow this psalm of lament to give voice to our inner anguish? What would it take for us to pour out our unedited reactions to life and circumstances to God?

HERE IS HOW I HOPE WE WILL ALLOW PSALMS OF LAMENT TO SHAPE OUR LIVES:

- Don't expect to offer to God only positive responses to life and to God. Instead be absolutely honest with God. Let it all pour out to our divine friend. Experience the healthy catharsis of being completely honest before God. Tell God about doubt, anger, and deep sadness. Even tell God about our self-righteous self-vindication. The psalmists did.

- Be deeply truthful to God about our sin as well as about our anguish and anger over our enemies. Since denial does not work with God, we should tell God the truth about how we really feel.

- Join with a long line of lamenters in praying this way. Learn from the psalmists to lament.

PRAYING FROM PSALM 22

My God, sometimes my life seems to move between a sob and a song.

There are times when I feel like you, even you, have abandoned me and are far from me.

I feel like there is no answer even from you in my distress.

I feel like an absolute nobody with people poking fun of me.

I feel surrounded by enemies and physically torn apart by my body ailments.

I feel awful! My horizon is populated by evil and enemies.

My God, you've got to do something!

And you are coming to my aid. I know that even in the midst of my distress.

So I sing of your deliverance.

I call others to join me in singing about your faithfulness

I sing to you in the community of your people.

I want everyone worldwide to know you as great deliverer and to worship you.

My thanks to you, my God, for helping me not to get stuck in the sobbing mode. But you lead me on a journey to where I choose to sing praises despite how I feel.

Amen!

PRAYING FROM PSALM 55

Loving God, how I thank you that the full gamut of human feelings may be honestly and openly offered to you.

You accept our feelings of complaint, anguish, fear, anger, and desire to escape.

You accept our feelings when we have been betrayed by a close friend.

You accept even those feelings I may be embarrassed to utter out loud.

Help me to learn increasingly how to vent to you when I am troubled, to pour out the full range of emotions to you.

Help me to learn increasingly how to cast all those burdens upon you, for you are the One who can and will sustain me.

Today I rest on this affirmation: "Cast your burden on the Lord, and He will sustain you."

Amen!

7

Psalm-Shaped Hope

> You, O Lord, are my hope,
> My trust, O Lord, from my youth . . .
> I will hope continually. (Ps. 71:5, 14)

FOR SEVERAL years, Norman Cousins was editor of the *Saturday Review*. He wrote about getting better from an incurable and painful disease through large doses of programmed laughter. In the last ten years of his life, Cousins became a professor at UCLA Medical School to document and teach his theories about the impact of our outlook on life on our physical health. One of his books is titled *Headfirst: The Biology of Hope*. Its thesis is that hope has biological impacts on the quality of life and even on its duration. Cousins urged people not to deny a diagnosis of a disease. But he did urge people to defy the verdict—the sentence of six months, a year, or two years or more to live. It is hope, Cousins affirms, that gives people life in whatever span of life they have left.[1]

Billy Graham has observed that it is possible to live a lifetime without sex. You can live maybe seventy-five days without food, ten days without water, and six minutes

1. Cousins, *Headfirst*.

without oxygen. But it is impossible to live very long without hope. "What oxygen is for the lungs, so is hope for the meaning of life," wrote theologian Emil Brünner.[2]

In contrast to hope, fear has become the most powerful emotion in today's world. Listen to Max Lucado in his book titled *Fearless*: "Fear, it seems, has taken a hundred-year lease on the building next door and set up shop. . . . Fear is the big bully in the high school hallway: brash, loud, and unproductive."[3]

Fear today is being promoted on the radio, on TV, sometimes even in church. Fear is whipped up by exaggerated claims of what will happen if we do or do not do this or that. Fear is whipped up by half truths that people buy into and become anxious over. Fear is stirred by wild stories of what happened when. Fear-mongering is particularly intense in political campaigns. A politician returned to Washington, DC, after an August of town meetings on health care issues. He said that what surprised him was not the anger but the fear he heard. We live in a world full of fear evangelists. Fear-mongering has become an art form in our day and age.

Often fear-mongering is directed toward those of us who are getting older. Wise Benedictine nun Joan Chittister writes, "Is there a future for me when I get old? Indeed there is. The future at this stage in life is tomorrow."[4]

2. Brünner, *Eternal Hope*, 7.

3. Lucado, *Fearless*, 3.

4. Chittister, *Gift of Years*, 162.

PSALM-SHAPED BELIEVERS OF ANY AGE ARE WARY OF THOSE WHO ROB US OF HOPE BY PUSHING FEAR ON US.

Immersing ourselves in the Psalms is a way to live with hope and trust instead of fear at any season of life. Hope-filled psalms are not so much a particular kind of psalm as a bright thread running through many of these spirit-shaping prayers. A psalm-shaped life is a life filled with hope leading to trust in God rather than being consumed by fear. Listen to the psalmist: "You, O Lord, are my hope, my trust, O Lord, from my youth. I will hope continually, and will praise you yet more and more" (Ps. 71:5, 7).

A psalm-shaped life is a hopeful, trusting life. Oh yes! We believe in Jesus and heaven and a future hope. And yes, that is true and good. Hope of a future with God is a powerful benefit to our lives today. But what about hopefulness for this life? What about an attitude of hope for all the seasons of life in which we find ourselves? Hope is for now, not just the hereafter.

SOMETIMES WE MISUNDERSTAND WHAT HOPE IS.

Sometimes when we think of hope we're really just engaged in wishful thinking. But that's not what the Bible calls hope. Ask a college student if she did okay on a mid-term. She may respond, "I hope so!" That's not biblical hope. That's wishful thinking. Ask a Seattle resident if it will be sunny tomorrow. "I hope so!" But that's just wishful thinking. Hope is not just wishful thinking that things will be better.

Hope in the psalms is also not just the absence of problems. In fact, the psalms are very realistic about circumstances, adversities, enemies. Many of the psalmists had a highly developed sense of the "enemy" that was voiced openly and angrily.

Hope, like faith, is not just "psyching oneself up," trying harder to look at the bright side. Rather, as N. T. Wright observes, "hope is looking at our situation and our own frailty in the light of who God is and what he has done for us. Hope . . . is not a vague optimism: it is looking at the future in the light of the same God and what he has promised to do for us, working his purpose out as year succeeds to year."[5]

HOPE IN THE PSALMS IS A VISION FIXED ON GOD IN THE MIDST OF LIFE WITH ALL ITS ADVERSITY AND UNCERTAINTIES.

Psalm-shaped hope is all about the psalmists' vision of who God is in the midst of trouble and adversity. Hope-filled trust is related to the Psalm's frequent reference to God as "refuge." With a faithful God as our refuge we can live in hope even in the midst of trouble.

> Protect me, O God, for in you I take refuge. . . .
> I keep the Lord always before me;
> because he is at my right hand,
> I shall not be moved. (Ps. 16:1, 8)
>
> In you, O Lord, I take refuge;
> let me never be put to shame. . . .

5. Wright, *Small Faith, Great God*, 31.

> Be to me a rock of refuge, a strong fortress, to save me,
> for you are my rock and my fortress. (Ps. 71:1, 3)

> Those who trust in the Lord are like Mount Zion,
> which cannot be moved, but abides for ever. (Ps. 125:1)

Very early in the Psalms, we encounter hope in the midst of trouble. Psalm 3 opens with an exclamation about the psalmist's enemies. Foremost among them, according to the psalm heading, was David's own son Absalom: "O Lord, how many are my foes! Many are rising against me; many are saying to me, 'There is no help for you in God'" (Ps. 3:1–2).

But then the psalmist refocuses his vision on God. "But you, O Lord are a shield around me, my glory, and the one who lifts up my head" (Ps. 3:2). This vision of God gave the embattled king-psalmist hope to trust and be at peace in the midst of his trouble. "I lie down and sleep; I wake again, for the Lord sustains me. I am not afraid of ten thousands of people who have set themselves against me" (Ps. 3:5–6).

Psalm 37 begins with human vision consumed with envy directed toward wrongdoers. "Do not fret because of the wicked" (37:1) is the exhortation. The opposite of human fretting is to "trust in the Lord . . . take delight in the Lord" (37:3–4). Out of this vision comes the hope-filled promise: "Those who wait for the Lord shall inherit the land" (37:9). Six times in Psalm 37 there is the promise of inheriting the land. The Psalmist's vision is shaped not by the wicked and their seeming prosperity but by trusting and waiting on God. This results in at least two hope-filled factors:

- There is a sense of *place*. I belong here. This is my

land. For God's ancient people, living on their land gave them a hope-filled identity. "You will live in the land and enjoy security" (Ps. 37:3).

- There is also the assurance of *provision*. In ancient times you had to have land to provide for the needs of your household. "Take delight in the Lord and he will give you the desires of your heart" (Ps. 37:4). By contrast with the wicked, who may prosper in the short term but in the long term "will be no more," are "the meek [who] shall inherit the land and delight themselves in abundant prosperity" (Ps. 37:11).

HOPE WAS POSSIBLE FOR THE PSALMIST BECAUSE HE LEARNED TO "WAIT FOR THE LORD."

Again and again in the Psalms there is the testimony of what happened when the believer "waited on the Lord."

> I waited patiently for the Lord;
> He inclined to me and heard my cry.
> He drew me up from the desolate pit,
> Out of the miry bog,
> And set my feet upon a rock,
> Making my steps secure.
> He put a new song in my mouth,
> A song of praise to our God. (Ps. 40:1–3)

Again and again in the Psalms there is the exhortation to others to "wait on the Lord." "Wait for the Lord; be strong, and let your heart take courage; wait for the Lord" (Ps. 27:14).

But some of us don't like to wait on anything, let alone on the Lord. What is "waiting on the Lord?" For one thing, waiting on the Lord involves taking time for God. "For God alone my soul waits in silence" (Ps. 62:1).

Waiting on the Lord also involves trust in God's timing. God's deliverance often isn't on our timetable. Biblical hope is what I am learning to call "undated hope." It doesn't have a date and a human timeline attached to it. "You, O Lord, are my hope, my trust, O Lord, from my youth" (Ps. 71:5).

A psalm-shaped hope emerges from a psalm-shaped vision of who God is and a life focused around this kind of God. Listen to another psalm of David, which focuses vision on God in the midst of trouble: "The Lord is a stronghold for the oppressed, a stronghold in times of trouble. Those who know your name put their trust in you, for you, O Lord, have not forsaken those who seek you" (Ps. 9:9–10).

Those who know God's name, that is, who God really is and what God is really like, are able to put their trust in this kind of God. Hope is connected with our vision, what the eyes of our spirit are fixed on. But sometimes our vision is fixed on problems rather than possibilities. Then, if our circumstances are adverse, hope dims.

In Psalm 73, the poet once again complains about the prosperity of the wicked. "When I thought how to understand this, it seemed to me a wearisome task" (Ps. 73:16). But the psalmist refocused his vision on God through time spent in "the sanctuary of God." A vision fixed on God and God's purposes changed his vision from frustration to hopeful trust.

Whom have I in heaven but you?
And there is nothing on earth that I desire other than you.
My flesh and my heart may fail,
But God is the strength of my heart
And my portion [my inheritance] forever. (Ps. 73:25–26)

You, O Lord, are my hope, my trust, O Lord,
from my youth. (Ps. 71:5)

And now, O Lord, what do I wait for?
My hope is in you. (Ps. 39:7)

Hope sees beyond circumstances to God. We fix our vision on who God is. We use the ancient words of psalms to give us voice to affirm our trust in this God.

But sometimes a hope-filled vision can dim with the passing of time. Rabbi Mendel boasted to his teacher, Rabbi Elimelekh, that he saw the angels that roll away the light before the darkness. In the morning he boasted that he saw the angel who rolls away the darkness before the light. Yes, said the older Rabbi Elimelekh to the younger rabbi, "In my youth I saw that too. Later on you don't see these things any more."[6]

Sometimes with the passage of time it is not just our physical eyesight but the vision of our spirit that dims. Long ago a shipload of travelers landed on the northeastern coast of America. We call them the Pilgrim Fathers. The first year they established a town site. The next year they elected a town government. The third year the town government planned to build a road five miles westward into the wilderness. But in the fourth year, the people tried to impeach their town government because they thought it was a waste

6. Quoted in Dillard, *Pilgrim at Tinker Creek*, 30

of public funds to build a road five miles west into a wilderness. Who needs to go there anyway? Hope is often dimmed by circumstances and the passing of time.

How can we use immersion in the Psalms to shape a hopeful life that trusts in God in the midst of life's problems?

WE CHOOSE HOPE OVER FEAR

Martin Luther's favorite psalm was Psalm 46. "God is our refuge and strength, a very present help in trouble. Therefore, we will not fear" (Ps. 46:1–2). Out of this ancient prayer, the fifteenth-century reformer wrote the great hymn sung by Christians of all ages and places: "A mighty fortress is our God, a bulwark never failing."

How often does the Bible urge us "Fear not?" One evangelist claims there are 365 exhortations against fear in the Bible, one for every day of the year. Maybe it's a few more or a few less. But the injunction "Fear not!" is all through the book including in the words of Jesus. Contemplative Richard Rohr claims, "'Be not afraid' is the most common single line in the Bible. Look for yourself if you don't believe me."[7]

Fear is destructive of health and spreads like an infectious disease. Hope is an antidote to fear. John Adams asked his old friend Thomas Jefferson if he would agree to live his seventy-three years over again. Jefferson replied in the affirmative. He said, "I steer my bark with hope at the head, leaving fear in the stern." Hope chooses against fear.

Max Lucado points out that fear never has written a symphony or a poem, negotiated a peace treaty, cured a

7. Rohr, *Everything Belongs*, 67.

disease, pulled a family from poverty or a country out of bigotry, never saved a marriage or a business. Hope, not fear, does that.[8]

When we hear talk radio or our favorite TV news channel broadcasting fear, telling us what we really should be afraid of, we can choose against fear-mongering. There are some voices I simply will not listen to. I change channels. I turn the radio off. These voices are promoting fear. Hope chooses against fear.

WE TRUST IN GOD RATHER THAN IN HUMAN RESOURCES.

Listen again to Psalm 71: "Upon you I have leaned from my birth; it was you who took me from my mother's womb" (Ps. 71:6). Listen to the trust expressed by Psalm 146. "Do not put your trust in princes" (Ps. 146:3).

A recent church bulletin typo had adjusted this psalm to "Do not put your trust in prices." Very contemporary! But it's "Do not put your trust in *princes*." I adapt that to "Do not put your trust in presidents." I suggest that we expect too much of our presidents. And when they don't produce like we expect, we become angry and lash out at them. But whom do we trust anyway? What does our coinage say? "In God we trust!" Is that really true?

> Do not put your trust in princes,
> in mortals, in whom there is no help.
> When their breath departs, they return to the earth,
> on that very day their plans perish.
> Happy are those whose help in the God of Jacob,

8. Lucado, *Fearless*, 3.

whose hope is in the Lord their God. (Ps. 146:3–5)

One day Martin Luther was blue and discouraged. His wife that day dressed in black. At Luther's inquiry about what her mourning attire meant, she replied, "Haven't you heard? God is dead." Luther apparently saw the absurdity of his attitude. God lives and we can trust in God.

WHILE WE CHOOSE TO TRUST GOD IN THIS LIFE, WE ALSO CHOOSE TO TRUST THAT GOD HAS GOOD PURPOSES FOR US EVEN BEYOND THIS LIFE.

Hope trusts that God has good purposes for us beyond this mortal life. The Psalms and the Old Testament as a whole are rather cloudy when it comes to life with God after death. But even in the Old Testament there are hints that God has good purposes for us forever. Psalm 49, which we will look at more closely in another chapter, speaks of death, which comes to rich and poor alike. But there is a shaft of light that shines through the psalmist's words about death. "But God will ransom my soul from the power of Sheol [the place of the dead], for he will receive me" (Ps. 49:15). God has good purposes for this life and beyond.

Did you see the movie *Sea Biscuit*? Three battered men and a horse come together in this mostly true story. Here's Red Pollard, jockey—too tall, blind in one eye, broken down in body. His parents abandoned him as a kid so he could race horses. The book says of him that "he was sinking downward through his life with the pendulous motion of a leaf falling through still air." His winning rate had dropped to a mere 6 percent. At age twenty-six, he and another jockey totaled their car. Now, no car, no money, no prospects! But Red and his buddy hitchhike to a racetrack in Detroit. In Detroit is a horse that owners, trainers, and racers had about given up on. Too small, too awkward, too lazy! Here's a trainer who barely spoke and avoided people. He was good at horses but not much else. And here's a horse owner who had once known poverty, had experienced a failed marriage, and whose only son had been in an accident. These three men and a horse come together in the context of a down-and-out nation in the throes of the Great Depression. A booming economy and high hopes had led to a huge bust and had devastated lives of many. Does that sound familiar? Some of the devastation was due to poor choices and bad financial judgment. But the bottom line in *Sea Biscuit* is that you don't shoot a horse just because he's down. You don't throw a life away just because it's banged up. Watch the movie and remember that hope can fill us even when circumstances are a mess.

Hope is part of a psalm-shaped life. A psalm-shaped life includes a *vision* of God that leads to hopeful trust and a *voice* to express individual and corporate trust in God.

BUT HOW CAN WE FOSTER THIS KIND OF PSALM-SHAPING TOWARD HOPE AND TRUST?

- Choose! Hope doesn't just happen. Hope is a choice. Hope is a considered direction of life.

Choose and keep choosing against fear and for a hopeful trust in God.

- Be still, sings Psalm 46: "Be still and know that I am God" (Ps. 46:10).

- Make time for quiet reflection on who God is, especially God as seen in the Psalms. A hope-filled, psalm-shaped life has regular, nourishing oases of quietness.

- Look toward the God of these ancient psalms. Let God and God's Son, Jesus, dominate our vision, not fear. "Wait on God" as the psalmists urge again and again. "O Most High, when I am afraid, I put my trust in you" (Ps. 56:2).

- Finally, be with people who hope and trust. Hope is contagious. And so is fear. Being with hopeful people encourages us to live in hopeful trust, not fear.

This world cries out for hope, genuine hope, hope offered in a psalm-shaped life. As psalm-shaped people let us be men and women of hope in a world filled with the opposite by immersing ourselves in the great worship songs of God's ancient people, which are songs of hope. "You, O Lord, are my hope, my trust, O Lord, from my youth. . . . I will hope continually, and will praise you yet more and more" (Ps. 71:5, 7).

PRAYING FROM PSALM 42–43

I thirst for you, God, satisfier of human longings.

I confess that sometimes I allow my desires to be satisfied from other things but you.

Yet I know how unsatisfying that is.

And underneath it all is the deep desire for you.

My soul thirsts for you, O God.

You are the one who is steadfast love by day and song by night.

You are the one who is light and truth.

You are the one whom I worship in the company of your people.

You are the one who enables praise even when I am "cast down."

You are the one in whom I hope and in whom I find my help.

"Hope in God," you tell me.

I want to do so, thus finding the capacity to praise even in the midst of downcast and difficult times.

I thirst for you, God, for you the living God.

I believe that in you are springs of water which satisfy me and flow out to meet the needs of others.

Amen!

8

Psalm-Shaped Wisdom

My mouth shall speak wisdom;
The meditation of my heart shall be understanding.
I will incline my ear to a proverb;
I will solve my riddle to the music of the harp. (Ps. 49:3)

Teach us to count our days
That we may gain a wise heart. (Ps. 90:12)

I USED to pray to make "right" decisions. "Lord, help me and help us to know the right thing to do." Now I pray to make "wise" decisions. "Lord, help me and help us to make a good decision based in the wisdom you have shaped and are shaping in us." Prayer toward a "right" decision implies that there is, in fact, one right thing to do. And we think God is responsible to let me know what to do. Prayer toward "wise" decisions accepts responsibility for living in the wisdom God desires to shape in us, and the responsibility for making decisions based on that kind of wisdom.

WISDOM IS AN ESSENTIAL PART OF A GOD-SHAPED LIFE.

The kind of life shaped by immersing oneself in the Psalms, both personally and corporately, is a life of growing in the

97

wisdom that comes from God. Do we lack this kind of wisdom? The Epistle of James urges us to ask for it with the promise that God does give wisdom generously and does not make us feel foolish for asking (1:5).

There's an entire section of the Bible we call "Wisdom Literature," including Proverbs, Job, Song of Songs, and Ecclesiastes. The New Testament Epistle of James sounds like Wisdom Literature. And Wisdom Literature includes some of the Psalms that describe concrete ways in which God wants us to live.

BUT WHAT IS WISDOM?

Wisdom in the Bible is not just being smart or intellectual. Nor is it obtained only by going to school. The wisdom that is from God is not just educated into us. The Bible, in fact, talks about a kind of wisdom that is earth-bound. According to James, this kind of wisdom is merely human in origin and is unspiritual—demonic, in fact. This "wisdom" that is not really wisdom results, says James, in "envy, selfish ambition, disorder, and all kinds of wickedness" (3:16). Though written almost two thousand years ago, James sounds remarkably contemporary. James's "wisdom" that is not really wisdom sounds very much like many contemporary worldviews and their consequences. (Pause for a moment and think of what passes for political and social wisdom today.)

Sister Joan Chittister describes the revolutionary vision of third-century leader St. Benedict. Chittister's book on St. Benedict is titled *Wisdom Distilled from the Bible*. Benedict called for hospitality in a time of barbarian invasion, for equality in a time of classes and castes, and for humility in a male-dominated society. But, says Chittister, the kind of wisdom St. Benedict drew from the Bible also "challenges our own world, too, whose heroes are Rambo and James Bond, military powers and sports stars, the macho and the violent." (Her heroes sound dated today, but you get the idea!)[1]

What passes for wisdom today usually involves power and information. And both power and information are most often translated into money. In *The Message*'s introduction to Proverbs, Eugene Peterson describes biblical wisdom as "the art of living skillfully in whatever actual conditions we find ourselves. It has virtually nothing to do with information as such."[2]

In our day we idolize IQ. But real wisdom is more like EQ, or "emotional quotient." Someone has observed that IQ gets you through school, but EQ gets you through life. While certainly not identical, EQ may be closer to what the Bible calls wisdom.

In contrast to this world's wisdom, James talks about the wisdom from above as first "pure, then peaceable, gentle, willing to yield, full of mercy and good fruits, without trace of partiality or hypocrisy" (3:17). This wisdom "from above" is from God, who, says James, gives it generously to humans upon our request (1:5). This kind of wisdom involves concrete ways in which God wants us to live in the nitty-gritty of every day life.

This kind of wisdom involves contrasts between blessed (wise) and cursed (foolish) ways of living and their

1. Chittister, *Wisdom*, 3.
2. Peterson, "Introduction."

consequences. "Whoever finds me [wisdom personified] finds life and obtains favor from the Lord; but those who miss me injure themselves" (Prov. 8:32–36). This kind of wisdom gives us not so much promises of what will happen if we live this way but statements of probable consequences. The oft-quoted proverb "Train children in the right way, and when old, they will not stray" (Prov. 22:6) is not a promise but a wise assessment of probability.

THE BOOK WE CALL PSALMS IS INTRODUCED WITH A WISDOM POEM.

Though the word "wisdom" is not specifically found in Psalm 1, it contrasts the person "who follows the advice of the wicked" with the person whose "delight is in the law of the Lord." The "wicked" are foolish even though they are wise in their own eyes. Men and women shaped by God's Law are the wise, the righteous.

> Happy are those who do not follow the advice of
> the wicked,
> or take the path that sinners tread,
> or sit in the seat of scoffers;
> but their delight is in the law of the Lord,
> and on his law they meditate day and night.
> They are like trees planted by streams of water,
> which yield their fruit in its season, and their leaves do
> not wither.
> In all that they do, they prosper. (Ps. 1:1–3)

By contrast, says the psalmist:

> The wicked are not so, but are like chaff that the wind
> drives away.

> Therefore the wicked will not stand in the judgment,
> nor sinners in the congregation of the righteous;
> for the Lord watches over the way of the righteous,
> but the way of the wicked will perish. (Ps. 1:4–6)

Wisdom segments of the Psalms speak not to God in prayer, but to listeners with wise exhortation.

> Come and hear, all you who fear God,
> And I will tell what he has done for me. (Ps. 66:16)

> Hear this, all you peoples;
> Give ear, all inhabitants of the world
> My mouth shall speak wisdom. (Ps. 49:1, 3)

THE FOUNDATION FOR TRUE WISDOM IS LAID IN THE FEAR OF GOD.

Psalm 111 echoes the classic statement in Proverbs 1:7: "The fear of the Lord is the beginning of wisdom; all those who practice it have a good understanding" (Ps. 111:10).

This "fear" called for by the psalmist and the wise person is not represented by a dog with its tail between its legs. The foundation of wisdom is not timid, scared-to-death fear. Rather, the fear that is the beginning of wisdom may be represented by a worshiper on his or her knees before God. This is the fear of respect and reverence.

So the psalmists urge:

> Now, therefore O kings, be wise. . . . Serve the
> Lord with fear. (Ps. 2:10–11)

> Let all the earth fear the Lord;
> Let all the inhabitants of the world stand in awe
> of him. (Ps. 33:8)

> O fear the Lord, you his holy ones,
> For those who fear him have no want. (Ps. 34:9)

One psalmist calls down a blessing on those who fear the Lord:

> Happy is everyone who fears the Lord,
> Who walk in his ways. (Ps. 128:1)

This core of wisdom is thus both attitude and action. It is reverence for God leading to life lived in ways that please God. A God-shaped life is a life molded by reverence for God. Thus Psalm 86 prays: "Give me an undivided heart to revere [fear] your name" (v. 11).

Psalm 19 along with the marathon Psalm 119 trace the impact of God's Law, or God's way of living, on the way we live. "How can young people keep their way pure? By guarding it according to your word. . . . I treasure your word in my heart, so that I may not sin against you" (Ps. 119:9, 11).

PSALM-SHAPED WISDOM HELPS US DEAL WITH TWO KEY ASPECTS OF LIFE: WEALTH AND DEATH.

Contemporary wisdom says there is nothing more certain in life than death and taxes. Death and wealth are two aspects of life addressed by the wisdom of the Psalms. What God has to say about these central aspects of life come together in Psalm 49. "Don't trust in wealth" is the wise exhortation of the psalmist. "And if riches increase do not set your heart on them" (Ps. 62:10). But why?

Wealth comes to some. But that should not unduly impress us. Wealth comes and it goes. But wealth cannot prevent death. We cannot buy our way into living forever. And all wealth comes to an end with death. "Do not be afraid ["overawed" NIV] when some become rich, when the wealth of their houses increases. For when they die they will carry nothing away; their wealth will not go down after them" (Ps. 49:16–17).

The Message paraphrase is especially apt: "Don't be impressed with those who get rich and pile up fame and fortune. They can't take it with them; fame and fortune all get left behind. Just when folks think they've arrived and folks praise them because they've made good, they enter the family burial plot where they'll never see sunshine again." Ever seen a hearse pulling a U-Haul? I didn't think so!

The wise man's thoughts move from wealth to death. Wisdom involves *trusting God's care even in the face of death*. Death is a part of human reality. Most days, news brings casualty figures for wars in Iraq and Afghanistan or from some terrorist event. During World War II, C. S. Lewis pointed out that war does not increase death; death is total in every generation. It takes every one of us. George Bernard Shaw quipped: "The statistics on death are quite impressive. One out of one people die."[3] Death *is* part of human reality. And we need to face its reality if we are to live fully. Eugene Peterson observes that "preparing for a good death has been, in every century except our own, an accepted goal in life." Psalm 90, he points out, has been part

3. Graham, *Death and the Life After*, 3

of that preparation.[4] "Teach us to number our days," prays the author of this wisdom psalm, "that we may gain a wise heart" (Ps. 90:12).

Even as we face death openly and wisely, we trust the God whom we revere and for whom we live. Again from Psalm 49: "God will ransom my soul from the power of Sheol [the place of the dead in Hebrew thought] for He will receive me" (Ps. 49:15; or "He will surely take me to Himself" [NIV]).

The same word is used of Enoch, of whom it was said "He was not for God took him, received him" (Gen. 5:24). *The Message* says, "God snatches me from the clutch of death, he reaches down and grabs me."

The older testament has a cloudy view of what happens after death. It is only in the New Testament that we have a fully developed view of the resurrection and the life everlasting. But out of this pre-Christian wisdom poem comes affirmation of trust in God's care even in the face of death.

In contrast to the eternity of God, Psalm 90, attributed to Moses, describes the transience of human life.

> You turn us back to dust,
> And say, "Turn back, you mortals."
> You sweep them away; they are like a dream,
> Like grass that is renewed in the morning;
> In the morning it flourishes and is renewed;
> In the evening it fades and withers away. (Ps. 90:3, 5–6)

> Lord, let me know my end . . . let me know how fleeting my life is.

4. Peterson, *Living the Message*, 305.

> You have made my days a few handbreadths,
> And my lifetime is as nothing in your sight.
> Surely everyone stands as a mere breath.
> Surely everyone goes about like a shadow. (Ps. 39:4–6)

Dealing with death confronts us with the reality that we were not made to live forever on this earth. The standard span of life according to Psalm 90 is seventy years, or perhaps eighty if we are strong (Ps. 90:10). Today, some people live to one hundred years and beyond. But none of us are immortal.

Eugene Peterson tells of visiting a Benedictine monastery in New Mexico with his wife. One of the brothers was leading them on a path from prayers in the chapel to the refectory for lunch. The path led through the monks' cemetery. Passing an open grave, Jan Peterson asked, "Oh, did one of the brothers just die?" "No, this is for the next one," was the response. Three times a day, on their way from praying together to eating together, the monks are reminded that one of them will be "the next one."[5]

It is in the context of acknowledging how transient human beings are that the psalmist prays for "a wise heart." "Counting" or "being aware of" our days, relatively few as they may be—seventy or perhaps eighty years—is part of being wise. "So teach us to count our days that we may gain a wise heart" (Ps. 90:12). Or, as *The Message* puts it, "Oh! Teach us to live well! Teach us to live wisely and well!"

Nearly three thousand years after these ancient wise men, what happens when we allow psalm-shaped wisdom to form our lives?

5. Peterson, *Pastor*, 289.

- We revere God. That is the foundation of our worldview.

- We obey God. Out of revering God comes a commitment to live in light of God's guidance for living. We believe that to revere God and obey God is to flourish in life.

- We trust in God amid all the circumstances of life, even when facing death.

Psalm-shaped wisdom formed how believers in ancient times looked at wealth and death. This same realistic but reverent and trusting wisdom can shape believers of the twenty-first century also.

PRAYING FROM PSALM 1

God of wisdom, you give us health-filled guidance for living.

You show us the way that is good for us to live.

And you show us the consequences for not living that way.

Thank you for marking the way for us to journey.

I want to delight in your law and meditate on it day and night.

I want thus to flourish and be fruitful like a tree planted by a river.

I don't want a withered, dried-up existence.

So enable me to live wisely, with your wisdom.

Thus, help me avoid the chaff-like life of those who ignore your wisdom.

Amen.

9

Psalm-Shaped Celebration

> Sing praises to God, sing praises;
> Sing praises to our King, sing praises.
> For God is king of all the earth;
> Sing praises with a psalm. (Ps. 47:6–7)

REMEMBER THE hand-clapping, foot-stomping, full-throated celebration modeled in *Fiddler on the Roof*? The wedding feast of Motel and Zeitel was celebrated with gusto. Jews of ancient times and of today know how to celebrate.

A PSALM-SHAPED LIFE GIVES VISION AND VOICE FOR TIMES OF CELEBRATION.

Psalm-shaped people of the twenty-first century, Jews and gentiles, celebrate! Milestones, sacred days, special events, remembrances, and many kinds of liturgies can be marked with joy and exuberance. At times celebration may be colored by loss and sadness, as when we celebrate the life of a good person who has died. But psalm-shaped people of God should know how to celebrate. Our ancestors in the faith who wrote the Psalms show us how.

THE PSALMS CELEBRATE THE KING AND HIS ACCOMPLISHMENTS.

When the king brought the ark to Jerusalem, the people of Israel celebrated. According to the writer of 1 Chronicles, "David assembled all Israel . . . to bring up the ark of God, the Lord, who is enthroned on the cherubim, which is called by his name. David and all Israel were dancing before God with all their might, with song and lyres and harps and tambourines and cymbals and trumpets" (13:5–8).

Psalm 24 probably reflects this very special event in King David's life. In what was likely the climax of his life, David sang and celebrated.

> Who shall ascend the hill of the Lord?
> And who shall stand in his holy place?
> Those who have clean hands and pure hearts,
> Who do not lift up their souls to what is false,
> And do not swear deceitfully. . . .
> Lift up your heads, O gates!
> And be lifted up, O ancient doors!
> That the King of glory may come in. . . .
> Who is this King of glory?
> The Lord of hosts,
> He is the King of Glory. (Ps. 24:3–4, 7, 10)

Today, where is "the hill of the Lord"? Who is today's King of Glory that we celebrate? Could it be that when we gather for worship, we enter "the hill of the Lord," and it is Jesus who is crowned as our King of Glory? Psalm 24 is traditionally used on Palm Sunday, when we celebrate Jesus's entrance into Jerusalem to the praises of his followers.

The Psalms celebrated the king's enthronement. To get a feel for this, non-royalist Americans need to imagine Westminster Abbey and the pageantry of our British cousins. The English celebrate the coronation of their kings and queens with high drama. Ancient believers in Israel celebrated their king. But they recognized that behind David and David's sons, God was really King.

Psalm 93, for example, celebrates the One who is really King. "The Lord is king, he is robed in majesty; the Lord is robed, he is girded with strength" (Ps. 93:1).

Psalm 47 conjures images of kingly enthronement and its celebration. But the king here is "the Lord, the Most High" (Ps. 47:2). This psalm is traditionally used to celebrate Ascension Sunday. On this Sunday, six weeks after the celebration of Jesus's triumph over death in the resurrection, we retell and celebrate the story of how

> God also highly exalted him
> And gave him the name
> That is above every name,
> So that at the name of Jesus
> Every knee should bend,
> In heaven and on earth and under the earth,
> And every tongue should confess
> That Jesus Christ is Lord
> To the glory of God the father. (Phil. 2:9–11)

THE PSALMS ALSO CELEBRATED VICTORY OVER ENEMIES.

It is no secret that the Psalms have a highly developed sense of "enemy," both personal and corporate. God is the warrior who delivers his people from their enemies. It is their Lord who delivered Israel. It is our Lord Jesus Christ who delivers his people today from bondage to the enemies of sin, evil, and death.

Psalm 98 celebrates God's victory in ancient times and gives contemporary believers vision and voice to celebrate the victory of Jesus over evil and death in his resurrection.

> O sing to the Lord a new song
> For he has done marvelous things
> His right hand and his holy arm
> Have gained him victory. . . .
> All the ends of the earth has seen
> the victory of our God. (Ps. 98:1, 3)

Psalm 98 celebrates not only what God has done, but what God will do.

> Let the floods clap their hands;
> Let the hills sing together for joy
> At the presence of the Lord,
> For he is coming to judge the earth.
> He will judge the world with righteousness,
> And the peoples with equity. (Ps. 98:8–9)

Isaac Watts's great Christmas carol celebrates what God has done in the coming of Jesus. But this is also a carol of the second coming that looks forward to the day when "He comes to make His blessings flow, far as the curse is found." Thus, while the Psalms celebrate the role and exploits of ancient kings, we use them to celebrate the King of Kings, who we believe is coming again in power and glory. While ancient psalms celebrate the defeat of the king's enemies, we may use them to celebrate God's victory in Jesus.

CELEBRATION PSALMS WERE ALSO USED BY PILGRIMS ON THEIR WAY "UP" TO JERUSALEM.

Psalms 120–35 are labeled "psalms of ascent." Today's visitors to Jerusalem catch some of the impact of arriving at the brow of the Mount of Olives and overlooking the holy city, now sacred to three religions—Judaism, Islam, and Christianity.

In his insightful treatment of these psalms of ascent, Eugene Peterson applies them to contemporary believers. "For those who choose to live no longer as tourists but as pilgrims, the Songs of Ascents combine all the cheerfulness of a travel song with the practicality of a guidebook and map."[1]

But pilgrim celebrations are not all "happy," and these psalms of ascent are not all "happy" songs. They express a life being shaped by our God in the midst of difficult times. In fact, these psalms reflect a kind of journey or progression through being bogged down in trouble (Ps. 124) to blessing the Lord and calling others to do the same (Ps. 134). Psalms 120–24 sing of trouble and the need for help; Psalms 125–29 sing of help and trust in the Lord; and Psalms 130–34 sing of security in the Lord.

Psalm 84, though not one of the psalms of ascent, is another song of pilgrimage. It reflects homesickness for God's temple and a desire to be on pilgrimage. "My soul longs, indeed it faints for the courts of the Lord. . . . Better is one day in your courts than a thousand elsewhere" (84:2, 10). The NIV continues the image of pilgrimage: "Blessed are those whose strength is in you, who have set their hearts

1. Peterson, *Long Obedience*, 10.

on pilgrimage. . . . They go from strength to strength" (84:5, 7). Even as they "pass through the valley of Baca [or "tears"] they make it a place of springs" (Ps. 84:6). Trouble and tears in our journey are transformed into blessing.

The life of a believer is a pilgrimage with God and to God. And traveling as pilgrims through this land to the next, we find ourselves caught up in whole-person, full-bodied celebration. "My heart and my flesh sing for joy to the Living God" (Ps. 84:2).

A psalm-shaped life is one of journey. And journeys carry with them the possibility of hazard and trouble. But the psalm-shaped journey is also one of joyous celebration because we know the One who walks with us and the One to whom we journey. Believers celebrate the presence of God now but also anticipate the more complete experience of God's presence at our journey's destination.

How can these psalms of journey and celebration shape our celebrations by giving a biblical vision and voice to these momentous times?

What would the impact of psalm-shaping be in our personal and corporate celebrations?

What if we were to celebrate with gusto but turn our celebrations not just toward ourselves and what we have done but to the Lord God, "from whom all blessings flow?"

Let these celebration psalms shape our celebrations of God and of life all through our human journey.

PRAYING FROM PSALM 84

How I thank you, Lord, for the homing instinct, even the homesickness for you, that causes me to long with the psalmist for you and for your presence.

I long to know your presence in my daily journey of life.

And when I encounter you in congregational worship or in my own openness to you, there is a whole-person joy.

My heart and my flesh do sing for joy to you, the living God.

How I thank you for strength that comes in journeying with you, strength that grows and goes from strength to strength.

I thank you, Lord, that in addition to joy and strength from you, no good thing will you withhold from those who walk uprightly.

You delight to give good gifts, to fill my life with your goodness.

O Lord, how happy are those who trust in you!

Amen!

10

How to be Shaped by the Psalms

> Be still, and know that I am God!
> I am exalted among the nations,
> I am exalted in the earth.
> The Lord of hosts is with us;
> The God of Jacob is our refuge. (Ps. 46:10–11)

> The righteous flourish like the palm tree,
> And grow like a cedar in Lebanon. . . .
> In old age they still produce fruit,
> They are always green and full of sap. (Ps. 92:12, 14)

IT IS my experience, both personally and with a congregation of believers, that the Psalms can powerfully shape how we worship and pray. When we are immersed in the Psalms, they shape our whole life before God. We experience psalm-shaped life. We become psalm-shaped people. This was so with the people of God in ancient Israel. This has been so in the church whenever the Psalms have been regularly and meaningfully used personally and corporately. The Psalms shape our vision of who God is and what God is like. And the Psalms shape our voice in response to this God, often giving us language to bring before God all of life's experiences.

For example, we open our eyes for a fresh vision of who God is in Psalm 36. And we allow the psalmist's words to give us powerful voice to respond to God.

> Your steadfast love, O Lord, extends to the heavens,
> Your faithfulness to the clouds.
> Your righteousness is like the mighty mountains,
> Your judgments are like the great deep;
> You save humans and animals alike, O Lord. (Ps. 36:5–6)

Central to our vision of God, opened up and repeated again and again in the Psalms, is what the NRSV powerfully renders as "steadfast love." This is the love of covenant between God and human beings. Whatever else God is, God *is* loving and faithful to God's covenant. God's righteousness and even God's judgments proceed out of God's steadfast love. The psalmist sees this saving love of God extending to all people and even to animals (Ps. 36:6). It is because of this covenant, this faithful love of God that we may "take refuge in the shadow of your wings, feast[ing] on the abundance of your house" (Ps. 36:8). It is out of this core, this divine heart that God allows those who do not trust him to reap the consequences of their own rejection (Ps. 36:1–4, 11–12). By contrast, it is out of steadfast love that God saves, delivers, and fills with good things those who know God and who are upright in heart (Ps. 36:10). Again and again, the psalmists' vision of God centers in the One who is "abounding in steadfast love" (Ps. 103:8).

Several centuries after the book of Psalms was completed, John, follower of Jesus and leader in the early church, again centers our vision of God squarely on the core of love.

Not only is love God's core characteristic, as expressed in Jesus, but that is the way God's followers should live.

> Beloved, let us love one another, because love is from God. . . . Whoever does not love does not know God for God is love. God's love was revealed among us in this way: God sent his only Son into the world so that we might live through him. In this is love, not that we loved God but that he loved us, and sent his Son to be the atoning sacrifice for our sins. (1 John 4:7–10)

Thus the vision of God centered in faithful love we see in the Psalms, the heart of the Hebrew Bible, is reinforced in the New Testament.

But returning to Psalm 36, listen as the ancient poet responds to who God is and what God is like. These powerful images give us voice to respond to God three millennia later. "How precious is your steadfast love, O God! . . . With you is the fountain of life; in your light we see light. O continue your steadfast love to those who know you" (Ps. 36:7–10).

The case has been made in this book that our vision of God is shaped by the Psalms as we turn toward this kind of God both individually and corporately. The case has also been made that the ancient words of prayer give us voice to join with the psalmists and God's people of all ages in responding to God in the midst of all the circumstances of life. Immersion in the Psalms does shape us powerfully. We neglect this means of spiritual formation to our personal and corporate detriment.

But with many contemporary believers, feeling of distance from some of the Psalms is off-putting. We're not sure how to deal with some of the intensity expressed so honestly and openly in the Psalms. We worry about whether it is okay to talk to God that way. Reacting to recent political upheaval in the Middle East, someone asked me, "Why are they so volatile?" My response: "Have you read the Psalms recently?"

Listen to wise words from Eugene Peterson: "With the Psalms we bring into awareness an ancient sorrow, release a latent joy. We use the Psalms to present ourselves before God as honestly and thoroughly as we are able. A mirror shows us the shapes of our nose and the curve of our chin, things we otherwise know only through the reports of others. The Psalms show us the shape of our souls and the curve of our sin, realities deep within us, hidden and obscured, for which we need focus and names."[1]

With many churches not guided by a lectionary schedule, the corporate reading of Psalms has been hit or miss. The outcome has been to limit the shaping impact of this powerful biblical resource. Could it be that spiritual life for many of us is more shaped by Christian self-help books than by the Psalms? Could it be that we go to easy-to-digest, quick-read devotionals (as valuable as they are) for a daily shot in the arm instead of to the Psalms?

So what do I urge on us as seekers after God and as communities of seekers after God?

READ THE PSALMS REGULARLY.

Read two or three psalms per day depending on their length and the time available. Read slowly, trying to identify with

1. Peterson, *Living the Message*, 277.

the emotions being poured out to God. Maybe a word or phrase will jump out at you. Savor that insight on God. Incorporate that voice for communicating with God into your own prayers.

READ ALL THE PSALMS.

Read the whole book of Psalms all the way through, including the angry and unhappy psalms. You will probably skip a day or two here and there. A pattern rather than perfect performance is what I am urging and what characterizes my own immersion in the Psalms. Build a new habit of reading the Psalms.

READ THE PSALMS TO ENCOUNTER GOD.

Read the Psalms not so much for information, but to encounter God. Read the Psalms to respond to who God is in the midst of whatever is happening in our lives. This is what believers over the centuries have called *lectio divina*, or spiritual reading. As Eugene Peterson describes it, this is "reading personally, not impersonally, reading for a message that affects who we are and are becoming the way we live our lives, and not merely for information that we can use to raise our standard of living."[2]

Henri Nouwen writes, "Reading in a spiritual way is reading with a desire to let God come closer to us. . . . The purpose of spiritual reading . . . is not to master knowledge or information, but to let God's Spirit master us. Strange as

2. Ibid., 312.

it may sound, spiritual reading means to let ourselves be read by God!"[3]

Before I begin my reading from the Psalms or from any part of the Bible, I pause and consciously turn my heart toward God. As I prepare my heart to encounter God often I use prayers from the Psalms, often a psalm's own opening prayer.

> To you, O Lord, I lift up my soul. (Ps. 25:1)

> As the deer longs for flowing streams,
> So my soul longs for you, O God. (Ps. 42:1)

> For God alone my soul waits in silence;
> From him comes my salvation. (Ps. 62:1)

> O God, you are my God, I seek you,
> My soul thirsts for you. (Ps. 63:1)

Spiritual sages urge us to read Scriptures slowly. If we move too fast we'll miss most of what is there. We should read imaginatively, not reducing the Bible merely to ideas, slogans, or principles, or to out-of-context, here-and-there verses. We read prayerfully, believing that "Bible reading is prayed reading." And we read obediently, accepting our task not only to read but to obey, believe, and trust.

Sometimes my daily reading from the Psalms will not seem to open up an encounter with God. Maybe it's one of those angry, bitter psalms, which, as we have seen, can be powerful at the right season and time of life. But this day I'm not angry at the Babylonians or any other kind of "enemy," or even angry with God. Sometimes when I reread the marathon Psalm 119, I can get lost in the length and

3. Nouwen, *Here and Now*, 95.

similar sounding petitions. While I am not surprised by "dry" days with the Psalms, I try not to skip any of them as I read through the book. If a psalm or psalms do not open up an encounter with God, I read on, or I choose to acknowledge God's presence by faith—not because I feel God close to me at that moment. Reading the Psalms is a life-shaping habit I choose to maintain regardless of the ebb and flow of my response to God through them.

READ THE PSALMS WITH UNDERSTANDING.

While we do not major in analysis and do not primarily focus on understanding, our reading of the Psalms *is* enhanced by some understanding of background and meanings. For example, in Psalm 133's symbolic description of the impact of unity on God's people, it is helpful to understand some things about Mount Hermon and its geographical location relative to "the mountains of Zion." Mount Hermon, in the far north of the holy land (now in Syria), is the highest point in the Middle East and blessed with heavy dew. Mount Zion, one of the hills of Jerusalem, on the other hand, is on the edge of the Judean Desert—semi-arid, with very little dew. God's blessing resulting from unity is as if the heavy dew of Mount Hermon were to fall unexpectedly on Mount Zion with the blessing of moisture in a semi-arid place.

It helps the reader to know that Psalm 77's reference to Leviathan pictures a great sea monster in ancient Middle Eastern pagan mythology. Does this mean the poet buys into this pagan worldview? No! The psalmist describes the defeat of Leviathan, this pagan image of power, by the God of Israel.

To foster basic understanding when reading the Psalms, I suggest using a study Bible with some explanatory notes. Or use a handbook on the Psalms such as *A Christian Handbook to the Psalms* by R. E. O White.[4] If you are looking for a basic but complete commentary on the Psalms to have by your side when you read, I recommend the two volumes by Derek Kidner in the Tyndale Old Testament Commentary series.[5] As a contemporary scholar puts it, "His [Kidner's] comments are brief, but they are clear and packed with insight. . . . This is the commentary I recommend most for laypeople who are interested in the psalms."[6] You may also find answers to basic questions on the internet.

But if you don't find an explanation in one of your available resources, don't let that hinder your reading. Don't get hung up on difficulties, which certainly are there. As a famous author once observed, it's not what I don't understand in the Bible that troubles me as much as what I do understand. With or without complete understanding, the Psalms are filled with rich visions of God that open up encounter with God.

While trying to hear the Psalms as they were first used, that is, for a 500–1000 BC Middle Eastern culture, be open to encountering God today through these ancient prayers. Eugene Peterson's renderings of the Psalms in *The Message* do not "sound smooth and polished, sonorous with Elizabethan rhythms and diction . . . but rather earthy and rough. They are not genteel."[7] Peterson's contribution to

4. White, *Christian Handbook*.

5. Kidner, *Psalms*.

6. Longman, *How to Read*, 166.

7. Peterson, "Introduction."

Bible readers is to give us something as direct and pointed in modern language as it was to its first hearers and readers. Sometimes when I've read a psalm in a classic version such as the New Revised Standard Version, I will turn to *The Message*, often finding that its contemporary and direct renderings foster encounter with God.

READ THE PSALMS AS PRAYER. IN OTHER WORDS, PRAY THE PSALMS.

Go back over a psalm once more. This time pray the psalm. Let its words and images lead you into your own open and honest responses to God. Maybe you will want to put your own reflections on your psalm reading into a prayer. I have modeled this approach by sharing some of my own psalm-based prayers at the ends of the chapters in this book.

Eugene Peterson first led me in not just reading but praying the Psalms. This sage pastor, teacher, and author writes, "Our habit is to talk about God, not to him. We love discussing God. The Psalms resist these discussions. They are not provided to teach us about God but to train us in responding to him. We don't learn the Psalms until we are praying them."[8]

Often praying a psalm is easy to do. Many psalms are clearly addressed to God (Ps. 139). Many segments of psalms are prayers directed to God (Ps. 142:5–7). Let these psalms give voice to our response to who God is.

Other psalms may be turned to prayer with slight adjustment. Instead of:

8. Peterson, *Answering God*, 12.

> The Lord is gracious and merciful,
> Slow to anger and abounding in steadfast love.
> The Lord is good to all;
> And his compassion is over all that he has made
> (Ps. 145:8–9)

Pray this segment of Psalm 145 this way:

> Lord, you are gracious and merciful. . . .
> Slow to anger and abounding in steadfast love.
> Lord, you are good to all;
> Your compassion is over all that you have made.

Practice praying the Psalms, not just studying them. Praying the Psalms will shape our vision of God and give us powerful voice to respond to God in all of life's circumstances. Praying the Psalms regularly will lodge some of these powerful responses to God deep in the heart and the mind. Even though you may not deliberately memorize them, you will find that some of these prayers become available to your memory at night, in difficulty, at any time and in any situation. Any time of day or night, we can pray the Psalms.

LET THE LANGUAGE OF THE PSALMS BECOME OUR LANGUAGE OF PRAYER, OUR VOICE FOR RESPONDING TO GOD IN THE MIDST OF LIFE.

As I urged earlier in this book, let this be so even with angry, bitter psalms and haughty sounding, self-vindicating psalms. Let all of life be poured out before the One who has remarkable tolerance for radical variations in our responses to God and to life. Let psalm fragments repeated again and again nurture a Godward vision and trust in God by day and by night.

> My soul clings to you;
> Your right hand upholds me. (Ps. 63:8)
>
> You, Lord, are my shepherd,
> I shall not be in want. (Ps. 23:1)
>
> You, Lord, are my light and my salvation;
> Whom shall I fear? (Ps. 27:1)
>
> O my strength, I will watch for you;
> For you, O God, are my fortress. . . .
> O my strength, I will sing praises to you . . .
> The God who shows me steadfast love. (Ps. 59: 9, 17)

Some of us may resist giving forethought to public prayers, wanting instead to be "spontaneous" and thus "authentic." But without forethought or the guidance of the Psalms, our public prayers can easily sound trite, with frequent repetition of phrases we have heard from others. Why not use psalm fragments to give voice to our public prayers?

FINALLY, READ AND PRAY THE PSALMS IN COMMUNITY.

As we have observed several times, the Psalms were designed to be used not just individually but in the worship of God's people. And when we read them as a community, we do well to read them antiphonally, as they were originally designed. Let them give voice not only to the up-front reader but to the whole community gathered in worship.

Some worship hymnals have a selection of psalms for congregational use. If these are not available to you, checking one of the lectionaries accessible online will help you select a psalm for a particular gathering. In the lectionary, weekly Psalm readings take their place with Old Testament, New Testament, and Gospel readings. The website BibleGateway.com will give online access to Bible passages. Psalms or segments of psalms may be set up for antiphonal or responsive use and then printed out on paper or used in powerpoint slides.

The apostle Paul urged his protégé Timothy, "Give attention to the public reading of Scripture, to exhorting, to teaching" (1 Tim. 4:13). Non-liturgical churches in the West have focused on exhorting and teaching but not the public reading of a wide range of Scripture. Urge those who plan and lead worship to give worshipers the privilege and opportunity of regularly reading together from the Psalms. When you gather with a small group, let the reading of a psalm together lead you into prayer. When local, national, or international news is distressing, find a psalm of lament to give voice to the community's anguish over what is happening.

Read the Psalms in community. As psalm reading has done for millennia, it will shape the life of your community and your worship together. Encourage your community not to miss this powerful, shaping influence. Let modern believers and the contemporary church return to the consistent spirit-shaping of the Psalter.

In conclusion, hear this exhortation from scholar and author Tremper Longman III: "Go to the Psalms when you are happy and everything seems right with you. Sing laments to God when your life seems to crumble. When God hears your prayer, don't forget to thank him for his kindness. When you are frightened, be encouraged by the psalms of confidence. Heed the psalms of wisdom. Above all, go to the psalms to be honest with God."[9]

PRAYING FROM PSALM 86

This morning, Gracious God, I echo the psalmist's words: "Incline your ear, O Lord . . . for I am needy."

I also want to echo the psalmist's orientation of life: "To you, O Lord, I lift up my soul."

Not focused just on my own neediness, or other "gods" that capture my attention, I want to fix my gaze on you, Lord, "good and forgiving, abounding in steadfast love, merciful and gracious, faithful."

Today and every day may my heart be undivided so I may "revere your name and give thanks to You, Lord with my whole heart."

Today, I need my vision and life to be psalm-shaped, God-directed, thanks-oriented.

Amen!

9. Longman, *How to Read*, 148.

Bibliography

"The Book of Psalms." *The Wesley Study Bible*. Nashville: Abingdon, 2009.

Browning, Elizabeth Barrett. *Aurora Leigh*. New York: Oxford University Press, 2008.

Brünner, Emil. *Eternal Hope*. Translated by Harold Knight. Philadelphia: Westminster, 1954.

Chittister, Joan. *The Gift of Years: Growing Old Gracefully*. New York: BlueBridge, 2008.

———. *Wisdom Distilled from the Daily: Living the Rule of St. Benedict Today*. New York: HarperCollins, 1990.

Cousins, Norman. *Headfirst: The Biology of Hope*. New York: Penguin, 1989.

Dillard, Annie. *Pilgrim at Tinker Creek*. 1974; repr., New York: Harper, 2007.

Geoghegan, Jeffrey, and Michael Homan. *The Bible for Dummies*. Hoboken. NJ: Wiley, 2003.

Graham, Billy. *Death and the Life After*. Nashville: Thomas Nelson, 1994.

Kelly, Gerard. *Retrofuture: Rediscovering Our Roots, Recharting Our Routes*. Downers Grove, IL: InterVarsity, 1999.

Kidner, Derek. *Psalms: An Introduction and Commentary*. Downers Grove, IL: InterVarsity, 1973.

Lewis, C. S. *Reflections on the Psalms*. New York: Harcourt, 1958.

Longman, Tremper III. *How to Read the Psalms*. Downers Grove, IL: InterVarsity, 1988.

Lucado, Max. *Fearless: Imagine Your Life Without Fear*. Nashville: Thomas Nelson, 2009.

McGrath, Alister. *The Passionate Intellect: Christian Faith and the Discipleship of the Mind*. Downers Grove, IL: InterVarsity, 2010.

Miller, Calvin. *Spirit, Word, and Story*. Dallas: Word, 1989.

Nouwen, Henri. *Lifesigns: Intimacy, Fecundity, and Ecstasy in Christian Perspective*. New York: Doubleday, 1986.

———. *Here and Now: Living in the Spirit*. New York: Crossroad, 1994.

Peterson, Eugene H. "Introduction to Psalms." *The Message*. Colorado Springs: NavPress, 2002.

———. *A Long Obedience in the Same Direction: Discipleship in an Instant Society*. Downers Grove, IL: InterVarsity, 1980.

———. *Answering God: The Psalms as Tools for Prayer*. San Francisco: Harper and Row, 1989.

———. *The Pastor: A Memoir*. New York: HarperOne, 2011.

Peterson, Janice Stubbs. *Living the Message: Daily Reflections with Eugene H. Peterson*. San Francisco: HarperCollins, 1996.

Rohr, Richard. *Everything Belongs: The Gift of Contemplative Prayer*. New York: Crossroad, 2003.

Smith, Alexander McCall. *The Charming Quirks of Others*. New York: Random House, 2010.

Warren, Paul Christopher. *The Hymnbook of the Ages: A Study Guide on the Psalms*. United Presbyterian Women, 1976.

Wesley, John. "Sermon 103: What Is Man?" Available at http://www.ccel.org/ccel/wesley/sermons.vi.l.html#vi.l-p0.3.

Westerman, Claus. *The Psalms: Structure, Content, and Message*. Minneapolis: Augsburg, 1980.

White, R. E. O. *A Christian Handbook to the Psalms*. Grand Rapids: Eerdmans, 1984.

Wright, N. T. *Small Faith, Great God*. Downers Grove, IL: InterVarsity, 2010.

Yancey, Philip. *The Bible Jesus Read*. Grand Rapids: Zondervan, 1999.